W9-BKE-894

SAINTS OFF THE PEDESTAL

SAINTS
OFF THE PEDESTAL

real
saints
for
real
people

AMANDA M. ROBERTS

ST. ANTHONY MESSENGER PRESS
Cincinnati, Ohio

Excerpts from *The Story of a Soul: A New Translation* by Robert J. Edmonson, ©2006, Paraclete Press, Inc. Used by permission of Paraclete Press, www.paracletepress.com.

Scripture citations have been taken from the *New Revised Standard Version Bible*, copyright ©1989 by the Division of Christian Education of the National Council of Churches of Christ in the United States of America, and used by permission. All rights reserved.

Cover by Mark Sullivan and Jennifer Tibbits
Book design by Jennifer Tibbits
Pedestal photo © istockphoto.com/Christine Balderas

Library of Congress Cataloging-in-Publication Data

Roberts, Amanda M.
  Saints off the pedestal : real saints for real people / Amanda M. Roberts.
    p. cm.
  ISBN 978-0-86716-800-6 (pbk. : alk. paper) 1. Christian saints. I. Title.
  BX4655.3.R63 2008
  282.092 2—dc22
  [B]

                              2008001478

ISBN: 978-0-86716-800-6

Published by St. Anthony Messenger Press
28 W. Liberty St.
Cincinnati, OH 45202
www.SAMPBooks.org

Printed in the United States of America

Printed on acid-free paper

08 09 10 11 12 5 4 3 2 1

To my family and friends
who continue to teach me the real meaning
of love, faith and devotion

CONTENTS

INTRODUCTION

After this I looked, and there was a great multitude that no one could count, from every nation, from all tribes and peoples and languages, standing before the throne and before the Lamb, robed in white, with palm branches in their hands....

"These are they who have come out of the great ordeal; they have washed their robes and made them white in the blood of the Lamb.

For this reason they are before the throne of God,
and worship him day and night within his temple,
and the one who is seated on the throne will shelter
them...."

—Revelation 7:9, 14b–15

Growing up, my salient question about the saints—those men and women who have gone before us whom the church officially declares are in heaven—was "who cares?" I didn't mean it disrespectfully; I just couldn't quite see their relevance to my life. In my mind the saints were a bunch of old people (even the ones who died young somehow seemed old), who had lived a long time ago. Life today was so modern and different; I just couldn't imagine their lives could speak to mine in any meaningful way. Besides, they were saints, which to me meant they were different, special, superhuman. I was sure it must have been easier for them to know and do the right thing. I was sure God must have sort of paved a smooth path for them so they could just breeze through life. I was just an ordinary, average person, struggling in a cloud of confusion and angst. What could the saints know about what it's like to wrestle with figuring out who you are, who you want to become, what to do with your life and what you stand for and believe?

I don't think I'm the only one who has ever felt this way about the saints. They seem to loom over us, standing larger than life on a pedestal beyond our reach, some of them growing larger with each passing century. What little many of us know about them makes us feel as if they stand in a category all their own, one to which we don't belong and could never hope to. Not only do they seem different than us, but they also are from other time periods, times that precede such things as easy travel, mass communication and modern technology, and it is easy to believe their lives are as obsolete as are so many things from back then. Busy as we are, we are happy to leave them on their pedestals, paradoxically both well and little known.

As we go about our lives, looking for direction, searching for guidance as we confront perplexing questions and challenges, it is unfortunate that we don't turn to these heroes of our faith for help more often. Looking to these men and women for insight into our own lives, we find that despite the fact that they didn't have things like computers and cars (and some of them would probably have loved to have them), even the most extraordinary among them is surprisingly and accessibly human. For none of the saints were born on the pedestal to which we have relegated them. They struggled to find and persevere in their paths just like the rest of us do. They faced internal weaknesses and external challenges just as we do. And at the end of the day they came through their ordeals, just like we can, just like we must.

In the pages ahead you will meet some of these great saints of our tradition whose stories take place in times gone by—some of them not so long ago—and places far and near. The stories of how these men and women became revered heroes are stories whose questions and struggles are still relevant and will always be so because they are the ultimate questions and challenges we all face. In these stories you will meet men and women who struggled to define their identity and character, discover their vocation and passion and understand the meaning and purpose of their lives while remaining true to who God called them to be. You will meet men and women who struggled to persevere with hope in the face of suffering, loss, failure, hardship and hostility. You will meet men and women who stood firm in their belief that God was with them, guiding them, even when others thought them foolish or worse.

Each story offers many lessons and insights and could offer more if more pages were dedicated to each one. After each story I share my thoughts on a particular aspect of the saint's life that I found most compelling and how it speaks to us today. It is my hope that these reflections and the questions that follow them will spur further thoughts and insights that help you, the reader, better connect the saints' stories with your own story of faith and shed light on the path you walk.

one

PETER

moving beyond failure

Pray that you may not come into the time of trial.

—Luke 22:40b

Peter is probably the saint we hear most about because there are so many Gospel stories that mention him. In all these stories this fisherman who became a disciple of Jesus of Nazareth sounds very much like one of us, alternating between shining moments and blunders, between getting it and missing the point altogether. No less susceptible to failure than the rest of us, his first real trial came during the passion of Christ when he denied and turned his back on Jesus. But Peter's story did not end in failure and the story of how he was transformed from the Peter too afraid to acknowledge Jesus to the Peter willing to die as a witness of Jesus offers us a powerful lesson of how we too can move beyond our failures to follow faithfully the path Jesus has set for us.

a fisherman from galilee

Peter grew up in a fishing village on the shore of the Sea of Galilee during the first century. A fisherman by trade, he worked alongside his brother Andrew in partnership with another family that included brothers James and John and their father Zebedee.

Fishing was an arduous profession. Peter and the others would work all night, physically throwing out and pulling in the net for hours in the dark, a risky affair in a sea subject to sudden storms. After working throughout the night, the fishermen would sort and salt the fish before taking them to be sold and mend the nets before hanging them up to dry. The hard work was not in vain, for it seemed the partnership was financially sound and provided a dependable income and respectable social status.

It was in the midst of fulfilling this daily work that Peter met Jesus.

Peter was one of the first disciples Jesus called to follow him in order to "fish for people" (see Matthew 4:19; Mark 1:17). Peter responded with enthusiasm and willingly left his livelihood behind. While reading stories like this from the Gospels, we probably can hardly imagine dropping everything to follow an unknown guru based on an obscure promise. But, given that they lived in an open society where everyone knew everyone's business, it is likely that Peter would have at least known about Jesus if not met him before. Saying that Jesus was not a stranger in no way changes the fact that the encounter must have made a powerful impact on Peter and offered a hope and vision he was hungry for to prompt the kind of radical change it did.

Peter was a married man, the breadwinner for his family, and any time away from his work would affect his family. Setting this responsibility aside, even for a season, meant resetting priorities, reinterpreting

> The region of Galilee lies north of Jerusalem, beyond Samaria. At the time it benefited from the commerce and foreign influence that came with being located along the Via Maris, one of the main trade routes of the Roman Empire that connected what is now Egypt to Iraq, Iran and Syria. But compared to the economic, political, and religious hub that was Jerusalem, Galilee was looked down upon as backwater country.

what he was about, and who his "family" was; there's no reason for us to believe it would have been easier for him to do this than it would be for us today. Yet Peter must have done some rethinking, must have come to see Jesus as family and participating in Jesus' ministry as a family obligation.

disciple of the lord

Most of us probably imagine Jesus and the disciples always on the move, with people flocking to their side wherever they went. However, being a follower of Jesus may not have been as glamorous as we might think. People in the first century were just as busy and involved in their own lives as people are today. Just as today people are more open and attuned to certain messages at certain times of the year, so it was in those times. During the dry season, when plowing and sowing were done and people were waiting for the crops to grow, people would have had more time on their hands, presenting a good opportunity for Jesus and his crew to travel through the countryside and "fish for people." That would leave the rest of the time for Peter, the other disciples and Jesus to stay home and possibly "fish for people" more locally while engaging in their regular work.

After what seems like a brief training period, Jesus sent Peter and the others off to carry the message of repentance and conversion with only a few basic instructions to do as Jesus had done: "Cure the sick, raise the dead, cleanse the lepers, cast out demons" (Matthew 10:8). And as to how they were to live while engaged in this ministry, they were to rely on the hospitality of those whose towns they visited.

So off they went.

Today in Capernaum, the village where Peter lived, one can visit what is believed to have been his house and get a better idea of what life must have been like for him. Veneration of this particular site has been constant since pre-Constantine times and nothing in the excavation itself has so far contradicted this identification, indicating the high probability that this was in fact Peter's house.

When they returned, Jesus took them aside so they could rest from their work and travel, or at least try to. But it seemed the work never ended—the crowds pressed on, and Jesus was a compassionate man reluctant to leave their needs unmet. Without missing a beat, we have one of the most memorable miracles—the feeding of the five thousand (without counting the women and children)—then more traveling, teaching and healing.

In all the stories that follow, Peter comes through as one of the closest disciples to Jesus (along with James and John), witnessing some events for which the other disciples weren't present—the healing of Jairus' daughter and the transfiguration—and later on, in Gethsemane, Jesus pulled the three aside and invited them nearer while they prayed.

Maybe it was his closeness to Jesus that also made Peter the leader among the disciples. Whenever the disciples are mentioned, Peter's name always comes first; whenever a big question is asked, Peter offered an answer, or when something was said, he came up with a unique comment—sometimes a good one and sometimes not the best one. Probably his most memorable good answer was the one he offered to Jesus' key question: "Who do people say that the Son of Man is?" It is Peter's response, "You are the Messiah, the Son of the living God," which prompts Jesus' blessing upon him:

> Blessed are you, Simon son of Jonah! For flesh and blood has not revealed this to you, but my Father in heaven. And I tell you, you are Peter, and on this rock I will build my church, and the gates of Hades will not prevail against it. (Matthew 16:13, 16, 17–19)

It is this blessing, regardless of whether Jesus expressed it in these exact words, that singled Peter out as leader among the twelve, as a leader of the community that would emerge, and that has given him a privileged role in our faith.

But at the time, Peter was a leader-in-training, a truth made only too clear by the fierce rebuke he got for the next not-so-good comment he made at hearing Jesus talk about his upcoming crucifixion. Just like that, Peter went from being a "rock" to being "a stumbling block to me... setting your mind not on divine things but on human things" (Matthew 16:23). Poor Peter, even after spending all that time with Jesus, after listening to all those parables and teachings and after witnessing all those miracles, he still didn't seem to get the picture.

In the eyes of the Roman authorities, Passover in Jerusalem was always filled with danger. Trouble was always bound to surface when thousands of people gathered in one city. The gathering centered on a religious feast that celebrated salvation from slavery—not the ideal feast if you're the occupying foreign power. In addition, in those times there were high hopes for a messiah who would free Israel from Roman oppression. For these reasons, extra troops were brought in to immediately and forcefully quell any potential uprising.

the passion

After spending some time in Galilee, Jesus and his disciples made their way to Jerusalem to participate in the feast of Passover. Jesus gathered his disciples for the Passover meal and for what turned out to be their final meal together. The mood at this meal was rather somber, and Peter became troubled by Jesus' announcement that one of them would betray him. Peter couldn't fathom that one of the friends he'd just dined with, celebrated Passover with, could act in such a way. His response was to affirm his own faithfulness to the end, even if that end was death, a faithfulness Jesus predicted he would be unable to keep. Unfortunately, when push came to shove, Jesus would be the one proven right.

After the meal, Jesus took his disciples to the garden of Gethsemane to pray as his hour of truth drew near. Troubled, he asked his friends to keep vigil with him, to pray to remain strong during the coming trial. But it was late. Peter and the others were tired and couldn't fully grasp what was coming and couldn't stay awake. Finding them asleep, Jesus woke them, urgently reiterating the need to stay awake and pray, but again they fell asleep. After he woke them a third time, the guards led by Judas arrived to arrest him. In John's account, Peter tries to defend Jesus using his sword only to have Jesus rebuke him for his outburst. While Jesus went willingly to face his fate, Peter and the others fled in fear.

The cold, dark night that had suddenly taken a terrible turn would only get worse. Along with another disciple, Peter went to where Jesus was taken, probably to try and find out what was going on. While warming himself by a fire, he was accosted, more than once, with accusations that he was in league with Jesus, that he too was one of the troublemakers. Cornered and beset, Peter denied, vehemently, the connection that could lead to his own condemnation, torture and death. Once the immediacy of the threat had receded, Peter remembered Jesus' prediction that he would fail to keep his promise to remain faithful. Realizing he had just done what had seemed unthinkable only hours earlier, Peter "went out and wept bitterly" (Luke 22:62).

resurrection

Fortunately for all of us, neither Jesus' nor Peter's stories end in such tragic failure. After the Sabbath, the women came back to where Peter and the other disciples were gathered with a fantastic tale about a stone rolled away, an empty tomb, a missing body and the news that Jesus had been raised from the dead. Peter and the others responded as most people would, even after going to the tomb to check things out: with disbelief and perplexity.

But disbelief turned into joyous faith through encounters with the Risen Christ. Probably the most poignant encounter between Peter and the Risen Christ is the scene by the Sea of Galilee we read about in John's Gospel. Peter and a few of the other disciples were back in Galilee, back to their regular lives and had gone fishing at night. Despite working through the night, they caught nothing. At dawn Jesus appeared on the shore, yet none of them recognized him. At the prompting of this stranger, even though they'd had the worst luck all night, they gave the fishing one more try and caught such an enormous amount that they could barely bring in the catch. It was at this point that one of the disciples recognized Jesus and shared his realization with Peter.

Peter responded by jumping into the water. Most of us imagine he must have been rushing to greet the Lord. Others suggest Peter was trying to get away—after what he'd done, maybe Peter wasn't ready to come face to face with Jesus. But Jesus greeted and invited all of them to come and have some breakfast by the charcoal fire he had going—a fire not unlike the one Peter had been warming himself at that terrible night. After they had all shared this morning meal, Jesus offered Peter the opportunity to reaffirm what he had denied, to be recommissioned as his follower and to be restored to his place in the community.

Various early church writings refer to Peter's travel to Rome and subsequent martyrdom in that city under Emperor Nero. The tradition that he was martyred head down can be traced to the writings of Eusebius, an early church historian.

apostle in the early christian community

For most of us, our knowledge of Peter ends with this scene in Galilee. But Peter's life continued, and he finally became the leader Jesus must have known he could be: courageous, fearless, with complete trust in the Lord.

It is Peter who suggests the apostles select someone to replace Judas—the one who had betrayed Jesus—from among those who'd also been with Jesus from the beginning. It is Peter, filled with the Holy Spirit, who proclaims the message of Jesus that converts the hearts of many on that first Pentecost. It is Peter who performs the first miraculous healing in the name of the Lord. It is Peter (along with John) who is first arrested for teaching about Jesus' death and resurrection in the temple. It is Peter who restores a fellow disciple to life as Jesus had done a young girl. And Peter is one of the critical figures involved in settling the first major dilemma this young community faced: whether or not gentile converts were obliged to follow Jewish Law.

Time and time again, Peter demonstrates Jesus wasn't so crazy after all in calling a fisherman from Galilee to be his disciple and appointing him leader of the pack. With a little help from the Holy Spirit (or a lot), Peter did what he had been unable to do before: He fully embraced the mission Jesus had entrusted to him. And when he was again questioned about his connection to Jesus, this renewed Peter did not turn tail and run. In fact, he was arrested for the crime of being a follower of Jesus more than once, and, as tradition holds, was ultimately willing to suffer and die as a witness of Jesus.

The church celebrates the feast of Saints Peter and Paul on June 29. The feast of Saint Peter has been celebrated on the same day as Saint Paul as early as the fourth century. The other principal feast connected to Peter is the feast of the Chair of Peter, celebrated on February 22, which commemorates Jesus' choice to have Peter sit in his place as leader of the church.

REFLECTION
the path to betrayal

Peter was one of Jesus' closest companions; so close, in fact, that they were like family. Like any friends, like any family, they most likely shared the type of lighter moments that bond people together. It was probably this closeness, this intimacy, that made it unthinkable for Peter to consider the possibility he might ever betray Jesus when the subject came up during that last supper. On the contrary, he was adamant he would stick by Jesus no matter what happened.

Unfortunately, that is where the path to betrayal begins for most of us, with that arrogant certainty that we're better than that, incapable of such a kind of disloyalty. Abandon our friend in their darkest hour of need? Pretend we don't know the person we've shared a venture with, not to mention countless meals and conversations? Leave a loved one to face the music alone? Lie to protect ourselves? Not us. We're good, decent people; we'd never get close to doing anything like *that*.

With this arrogant certainty that we would never do anything terrible, we fall asleep, figuratively speaking, like Peter and the others fell asleep. Like them, we remain unaware of the darkness that is coming our way. We fail to understand and see the signs that betrayal is much closer at hand, much more likely than we imagine. We brush aside the small red flags that have peppered our road with what become our mantras: It's nothing. I can handle it. It's not going to affect me. I'm not going to do anything bad.

And then things begin to take a turn for the worse and we react to them instinctively. Like Peter, when backed into a corner, we say the first thing that comes to mind that'll give us a safe way out; when confronted, we lie and just try to get out of the mess. By the time all the chips have fallen, we look back stunned at what happened. We can see ourselves through the situation. We can remember our actions and words, yet we feel somehow dissociated from them, as if someone else took over and did those awful things, but not us. How could it have been us? We're good people and good people don't do these things!

the path to forgiveness

On the heels of this betrayal, Peter wept bitterly as he realized he had done exactly what he had vehemently denied he could ever do. When we fall as Peter did, one of the things that can be hardest for us to swallow as we look back is how easily and quickly we fell, how vulnerable we were to the storms that brewed around us. We realize that all it took was the shadow of pain and suffering to hover over us for us to crumble and become what we swore we never would: people who betray their loved ones, their principles, their beliefs.

As we look around at the quagmire into which we have fallen, initially it may seem impossible to get out, to ever feel clean or whole again. It is easy to despair and be filled with self-loathing and endless self-recrimination, to feel compelled to punish ourselves for the wrong we did, to feel unfit or undeserving of any happiness because of this one, big mistake.

But Peter's story with Jesus shows us a better path, the path that Christ wants us to take, the path of forgiveness, healing and reconciliation. After Jesus' death Peter went back to the life he had before becoming a follower of Jesus. Maybe he felt it was all over now. Maybe he felt he couldn't go on alone. Maybe he felt he shouldn't go on in light of what he'd done. But the Lord was not yet done with Peter, and he sought him out in the place he had taken refuge. Jesus didn't come with accusations or recriminations, although they would have been warranted. Instead he stepped in with a miracle that reminded Peter that God's grace is as bountiful as the catch of fish, that God can fill our empty hearts. He stepped in with a meal he himself prepared to share with his friends, a meal reminding Peter that in the presence of our Lord, by the fire of God's love, our failure can be cleansed and forgiven, and our life can regain purpose and meaning.

When we take refuge in the familiar places and activities of our lives, Christ also seeks us out, prepares a meal for us, and waits to say those words of forgiveness we so desperately need to hear. Knowing that the Lord is waiting for us, we can jump out to meet him as Peter did, or we can remain out in the water, watching, preferring to remain in the shadow of the failure that has become a comfortable friend to having our darkness exposed and embracing the challenge of a new beginning.

the fruit of reconciliation

Forgiven and reconciled, Peter took advantage of his fresh start, of his second chance. He took to heart Jesus' mandate to follow him and allowed the Lord to show him what he needed to do and where he should go. No longer relying on his own strength—which had proven to be weaker than expected—but on the power of the Holy Spirit, Peter set out to continue Jesus' ministry. Peter's actions from then on are a testimony to the fact that when the source of our strength is in God, there is nothing we can't face.

Soon enough Peter would face incarceration and a constant threat of violence that would ultimately claim his life. But even though the threats that had once paralyzed him persisted, Peter would never again deny the Lord, never again seek to escape being cornered by betraying what he stood for and what he believed.

Like Peter, we are all capable of doing what seems unthinkable when we start to forget that we need God to strengthen us during our trials, when we fall asleep and stop being vigilant. But fortunately for us, our failures don't have to be the end of our story. God always reaches out to us with forgiveness, with another chance to do better. God always strengthens us in the Spirit as we embrace our new beginning. All we have to do is bring our boat in and follow the path Christ sets out for us.

REFLECTION QUESTIONS

How do you deal with your own failures and weaknesses? Do you fall prey to self-loathing and self-destructive behavior? Or do you confront and accept the darkness of your heart, finding comfort in the Lord's unconditional love and forgiveness?

How do you experience God's abundant grace? Do you come out to share the meal Christ has prepared for you in the Eucharist? Do you come out to experience Christ's forgiveness and reconciliation in the sacrament of penance?

Do you embrace the second chances you're given with a full and open heart, truly ready to do the Lord's will, whatever that will might be? Or are you only willing to embrace this chance so long as things don't get too hard?

How do you remain vigilant and attentive to the signs that might lead to situations of trial and temptation? Where do you turn for strength when these situations are upon you?

two

AUGUSTINE OF HIPPO

searching for the "real thing"

Again, the kingdom of heaven is like a merchant in search of fine pearls; on finding one pearl of great value, he went and sold all that he had and bought it.

—Matthew 13:45–46

From his youth, Augustine had ambitions of success and recognition. As he pursued a career that could lead to a governorship, Augustine simultaneously engaged in another pursuit he was even more passionate about: the search for ultimate truth and meaning. After years of study and intellectual exploration, Augustine eventually recognized the truth of Christianity and was finally able to embrace it through a powerful experience of grace. This conversion proved a turning point in Augustine's life. Following his baptism, he abandoned his career path for a quiet monastic life until he was pressed into service in Hippo first as priest and ultimately as bishop. As bishop Augustine responded to many of the challenges that assailed the church and society, remaining a beacon of light that continued to enlighten Christians long after

By his own admission, Augustine was not exactly the model child: "I told endless lies to my tutors, my masters and my parents: all for the love of games, the craving for stage shows, and a restlessness to do what I saw done in these shows.... Even in games, when I was clearly outplayed I tried to win by cheating, from the vain desire for first place. At the same time I was indignant and argued furiously when I caught anyone doing the very things that I had done to others. When I was caught myself, I would fly into a rage rather than give way."[1]

his death. We may not all share Augustine's genius, but most of us share his hunger for purpose and meaning, one that will only be satisfied if, like him, we are willing to dedicate the time and effort to the search for truth.

early years in thagaste

Augustine was born on November 13, 354, in Thagaste, in the North African region of the Roman Empire—now the Algerian-Tunisian border. His parents, Monica and Patricius, discerned his genius early in his life, and although they were not wealthy, they made economic sacrifices in order to provide him with the best possible education. Both mother and father were united in their desire to see Augustine rise beyond their current situation—a governorship was not out of the question—and Augustine's very name (meaning "little Augustus" or "little emperor") reveals their lofty ambition.

In keeping with this ambition, after beginning his studies in Thagaste, Augustine was sent to Madauros—some thirty miles away— to continue his education, returning at sixteen when the money ran out. Intelligent and well-educated, Augustine was nonetheless a teenager with nothing to do, and as always, this proved a bad combination. Falling in with the local fast crowd, Augustine struggled to fit in and impress his companions with his exploits: "[W]hen I lacked opportunity to equal others in vice, I invented things I had not done, lest I might be held cowardly for being innocent, or contemptible for being chaste."[2]

While with this rowdy company Augustine committed what he later considered a worse offense than any of his escapades: the purposeless theft of pears. What troubled him the most about this seemingly innocuous incident was that he had committed this pilferage only because it was forbidden; no other purpose was served except for the satisfaction of doing something evil simply for the pleasure of doing something evil, and that, to the Augustine who looked back on his life, was the gravest type of sin.

carthage, where the search begins

Augustine's days of leisure didn't last long. He was soon sent to continue his studies in the larger city of Carthage (in present-day Tunisia). Free to taste every pleasure the city had to offer, he did so with the unbridled passion of youth. But soon enough he met and settled down with the woman he would share a bed with faithfully for fifteen years and who became the mother of their son, Adeodatus. He never married her because she lacked the wealth and status to advance Augustine's career.

In terms of his studies, Augustine's focus was rhetoric—the art of speaking well. He excelled as a student and he enthusiastically pursued his hunger for knowledge. His reading led him to Cicero's *Hortensius,* a book that shifted the direction of Augustine's studies by awakening in him the awareness that the content of what is said is just as important as the way it is said. So began Augustine's lifelong pursuit of truth, the only content that truly mattered to him.

His search for truth first led him to the Bible. Augustine had not been baptized and, although his mother was a Christian and had taken him to church, he did not know much about Christianity. His first foray into Scripture shocked him. The classically educated young man was appalled by what he regarded as inferior writing. Despite what he had learned from reading Cicero, he was unable to look past the way things were written to consider the content and turned away from its words in disgust.

Still searching for answers to his questions, Augustine found his way to a belief known as Manichaeanism. What drew Augustine to this sect was its answer to the problem of evil. Manichaeans maintained that human beings had a dual nature—one good, one evil—at war

While teaching in Thagaste, Augustine suffered the death of a close friend. It was this unbearable loss that prompted his return to Carthage: "My heart was black with grief. Whatever I looked upon had the air of death.... The things we had done together became sheer torment without him. My eyes were restless looking for him, but he was not there. I hated all places because he was not in them.... I had no delight but in tears, for tears had taken the place my friend had held in the love of my heart."[3]

with each other and that evil acts were the work of one's evil nature. A decade later Augustine would see this argument simply as a convenient excuse he latched on to in order to avoid assuming moral responsibility for his actions. But at the age of nineteen, Augustine was hooked.

While embarking on his quest for ultimate truth, Augustine continued his studies and eventually began making a living by teaching, first back in Thagaste and then in Carthage. It was during this time that he forged several lifelong friendships. Prominent among them were Nebridius and Alypius, with whom he would share his agonizing search.

the crossroads in milan

Becoming frustrated with the unruliness of his students and the overall education system in Carthage, Augustine responded to the urging of friends to join them in Rome. They assured him he would find teaching in this great city a vast improvement in terms of remuneration and prestige, not to mention opportunities for advancement. But Rome turned out to be quite a disappointment, particularly since students often skipped out on a teacher *en masse* in order to avoid paying him. So Augustine lost no time in securing a teaching post in Milan. There his career finally seemed to be opening up the bright future he and his parents had dreamed about, for in addition to teaching, Augustine's job included duties as official orator. Giving speeches at official functions was just the kind of opportunity that offered the exposure and recognition to potentially open doors to better and higher positions. Despite the enormous pressure and misery he felt while preparing his first speech, Augustine was determined to remain on course.

Outwardly everything seemed to be coming together for Augustine, but he was tormented by the apparent emptiness and meaninglessness of it all. Before leaving Rome, Augustine had finally parted company with the Manichaeans. He had grown increasingly disenchanted with them, finding that his continued learning raised more and more questions not even their purported masters could answer to his satisfaction. Having abandoned the Manichaean belief system for good, Augustine's search for the ultimate truth about life intensified. This search led him back to Christianity, by way of Ambrose, bishop of Milan, whose openness, knowledge, intellect and eloquence appealed greatly to Augustine.

But intellectual questions still blocked the path to faith, so Augustine continued his philosophical reading until he finally found a satisfying answer to the question of evil that had haunted him for so long. Evil, he concluded, was not a matter or a force in and of itself as the Manichaeans argued; rather, it was a consequence of the gift of free will: Evil was the consequence of our failure to act righteously and our evil actions were our own doing, not the doing of some alternate nature within us.

The intellectual roadblocks to his conversion to Christianity were now lifted, but Augustine still felt unable to embrace it in his heart. He had grown convinced of the truth of the parable of the pearl of great price: A true Christian should be willing to leave all else behind for the love of God. But much to his distress, Augustine was unable to leave behind the pleasure of a sexual relationship. For anyone else, marriage would have been an acceptable option, but for Augustine, such a path would have ratified his failure to surrender completely to God. Nothing expresses his internal conflict better than his own words: "Grant me chastity and continence, but not yet."[4]

Still gripped by a divided heart, Augustine heard two powerful conversion stories that intensified his turmoil. Finding some privacy where he could weep away his anguish, Augustine desperately prayed for help.

Hearing the words, "Take and read, take and read," maybe from children playing, he took these words as a divine command to read from Scripture. He read the first words that jumped to his eyes: "Not in rioting and drunkenness, not in chambering and impurities, not in contention and envy, but put ye on the Lord Jesus Christ and make not provision for the flesh in its concupiscenses."[5] The words calmed his turbulent heart and in them he found the strength he had lacked to take that final step and embrace God with his full heart. At the age of thirty-two, Augustine gave up his post and after a rigorous period of preparation, was initiated into the church during the Easter Vigil in April of 387 along with Alypius and Adeodatus.

return to north africa

Having closed the doors to all those career opportunities he had aspired to for so long, Augustine and his enclave returned to Thagaste, where they settled in his home of birth in a monastic style community where he envisioned living out the remainder of his days. A quiet life compared with the life of his youth, Augustine filled his days discussing theological questions with his companions and corresponding on these matters with distant friends. Soon Augustine's writings began circulating to a wider audience and as they did, his reputation for wisdom in the faith grew and spread.

In Africa, the church was growing in many theological directions with various competing schools of thought. The church desperately needed leaders who could address the questions of the times. Such leaders were in high demand, but unfortunately, not in high enough supply. This led to a practice that put men such Augustine on the alert: When an area did not have a bishop, the faithful could press anyone into service, as had happened to Ambrose. Not wanting to abandon his quiet life in Thagaste, Augustine grew cautious in his travels, avoiding cities without a bishop.

But Augustine's caution was not enough. Responding to a friend's interest in the monastic life, Augustine traveled to Hippo (in modern-day Algeria) to help him make a decision. While there, Augustine found himself in church when the bishop—unaware of Augustine's presence—announced his need for help. Some of the gathered faithful recognized Augustine and brought him before the bishop, who promptly ordained him. Augustine burst into tears as he saw the quiet life he'd planned vanish, replaced by what he knew would be a demanding life of weighty responsibility and no rest.

Augustine quickly became Bishop Valerius' right hand, responding masterfully on multiple fronts to the various controversies in Hippo. Concerned that another town would still claim him for their bishop, Valerius persuaded Augustine to become his coadjutor. When Valerius died soon after, the forty-year-old Augustine became the official spiritual leader of Hippo.

bishop of hippo

As bishop, Augustine was a much sought-after preacher. His transcribed sermons reveal that this brilliant academic was also deeply concerned with the problems of the "little people"—heavy taxation, social stratification and eventually the slave trading that began to hit closer and closer to home. Impassioned and inspiring, his words could move his listeners to tears as he called them to task on their conduct and contrasted such shortcomings to the beauty, forgiveness and greatness of God's love for us.

In addition to all his duties as a bishop, Augustine was tireless in addressing the controversies that assailed the church through his correspondence and treatises on matters of doctrine. These multiple controversies became a vehicle through which Augustine defined and refined doctrinal positions on central matters of

Augustine would have been very aware of the practice of pressing candidates into service, for such had been Ambrose's fate. The well-connected young governor of the province of Milan had arrived at the city's church to resolve a dispute that arose upon the bishop's death. In resolving the matter he so impressed the assembly that its members acclaimed him as their new bishop.

faith, including the Trinity, grace, free will and sin, original sin and con-cupiscence. There was no time for all this work during the daytime, so Augustine devoted his nights to dictating these writings to his scribes. It is a testament to his genius that he had to plan out his high-caliber works in his mind before speaking them in the way he wanted them written.

He wrote his *Confessions*—probably his most accessible and most widely read work—in response to a request from a fellow Christian. The request, originally made to Alypius, who was now bishop of Thagaste, was for a work that would tell the author's faith story in a way that would edify the reader on the good Christian life. Although such autobiographical writing was not uncommon at the time, Augustine's turned out to be of a different mold in that it is a true confession of the heart, an honest and open look at both the dark and the light recesses of his soul. It was a courageous move, for it provided ammunition to his enemies, but Augustine undertook it hoping it would enlighten readers as to what can transpire when one is open to God's grace.

In 430 when Augustine was seventy-five, the turbulence that had begun to erode the strength of the empire came to his doorstep. Vandals surrounded the city of Hippo and began a siege. Three months later amidst the siege, Augustine fell ill and passed away. At the time of his death, the possession Augustine was most concerned about preserving for future generations was his library of books. Miraculously, his extensive works did survive and continued to illuminate for centuries the church Augustine had worked so hard to protect.

Augustine, doctor of grace, was added to the canon of saints when the process was still in the hands of local bishops and occurred in a more fluid manner as a result of local popular devotion. His feast day is celebrated on August 28, the anniversary of his death and entry into eternal life. He is the patron of theologians, sore eyes, printers and brewers and several dioceses.

REFLECTION
the search for meaning

Although we all share Augustine's capacity for reflection, some of us seem much more disposed to seek continuously for satisfying answers to the deeper questions of life, answers that will bring peace of mind and understanding, that will reveal the meaning and purpose of one's life. Others seem content to smother this natural inclination with activities and duties that leave no time or energy to ponder any question of substance.

Whether or not we take the time to reflect on the direction and meaning of our lives, until we come up with our own answer, most of us tend to follow the path set before us by society and begin moving through life's milestones: school, work, promotions, raises, dating, marriage and major purchases. As we move ahead, reaching milestone after milestone, in the eyes of the world we're a success story—we are on our way to having it all—and everyone keeps telling us how lucky we are and how great we must feel: young, our whole lives ahead of us, endless possibilities, all that good stuff. But in our hearts, in the corners we may never care to examine, we don't feel truly satisfied or happy; some of us even feel depressed, empty or adrift. Some of those achievements that are supposed to be crowning moments of our lives are wonderful and we feel great about them, but others seem sadly unimportant in retrospect, and the constant through them all is that none of them deliver the panacea of happiness promised. We still hunger for more.

the answers of the world

Augustine spent his fair share of time pondering the deeper questions about life and its meaning while going about his business of making his mark in the world. A committed seeker, he read and learned extensively in his quest for answers to the big questions that troubled him most: What is the nature of evil? Of the human person? What is the ultimate truth and meaning of life? His spiritual search brought him under the spell of one of the popular philosophical movements of his day. The Manichaeans had snazzy rhetoric and answers that appealed to him, probably because they were the answers he wanted to hear and didn't challenge him to question his behavior, interests or pursuits. They were a feel-good group.

The Manichaeans may not be around today, and although the contemporary feel-good proponents don't necessarily take the shape of a formalized group, there is certainly no lack of them. There are indeed so many of them, we are sure to find one or any combination of them appealing. For they all have their appeal, the myth that speaks to a dimension of our being, to our human desires, and which draw us by telling us things we want to hear. We may not buy into any of them completely, but we dabble in most of them to a lesser or greater degree at different times in our lives.

Here are a few that come easily to mind. The economic group: We are producers and consumers in a material world and the one with the most toys, the most money, the most power is the best and winner of the game. We may not be so completely materialistic, but who among us doesn't like his or her stuff and enjoying "the good life"? The romantic group: We are lovers in search of our soul mates and the ones who find a mate enjoy blissful happiness and fulfillment and the ones who don't find a mate, well, don't. We may not all be driven serial daters, but who doesn't want love and friendship in his or her life, someone who "gets you"? The beautiful people group: We are objects in a sex-driven, beauty-glorifying, death-denying society, and the ones who inspire the most admiration, attention and jealousy, and who remain young-looking the longest, are the winners. We may not spend *all* our free time between the gym, the spa and counting calories or carbohydrates, but who doesn't spend *some* time trying to look and feel beautiful? The survivor group: If you want to move ahead, you need thick skin and the willingness to do whatever it takes; the one who "outwits, outplays, outlasts" is the crowned winner. Most of us aren't this Machiavellian, but who doesn't hate seeing someone less gifted or qualified get the prize because they were willing to scheme and deal and we weren't?

the pearl of great price

Only after years with the Manichaeans was Augustine able to see the holes in their philosophy, the emptiness behind the glamour. As his disenchantment with them grew, so did his interest in another answer. With study, discussion and reflection, Augustine discovered a story that offered satisfying answers and filled his hunger. Unless we are willing to allow the world to define our lives for us, it is just as critical that we too ponder, reflect upon and examine the answers to the particular questions that plague our hearts. Only if we engage in this search will we too come to know with our heart and mind the pearl of great price which truly satisfies our hearts and brings meaning to our lives.

But the struggle is not over once we have found this great pearl. Fully embracing the mystery of our faith can prove just as much of a challenge, for its answers are not always the ones we want to hear, not always answers we like, clash as they do with the sins we hold on to and have become ensnared by, the ones we so masterfully explain away. In whose heart doesn't Augustine's prayer resonate: Free me of my sin, but not yet? Moving from the comfort of your old life to a new and yet to be revealed one can be a challenge some of us never get past.

But those who like Augustine find the courage to take this pearl with both hands and discover a meaning and purpose to life that is far richer, greater, more beautiful and loving than previously imagined; those who take the leap as Augustine did discover that the hunger of their souls can be satisfied; those who hold on to the pearl with both hands through the storms that are certain to lie ahead, as Augustine did, discover that despite the trials, in this pearl their heart is finally at peace.

REFLECTION QUESTIONS

What are your answers to the ultimate questions of life: Why are you here? What does it mean to be human? What is your purpose? What is the meaning of existence? What is the difference between what you say are your answers and what your actions, behavior and choices reveal are your answers?

Which myths, or answers, the world offers to the ultimate questions of life do you find appealing? What appeals to you about them? Which myths of the world influence your daily life and the direction you find your life heading?

What are the roadblocks that prevent you from fully embracing your faith and living as God calls you to?

three

FRANCIS OF ASSISI
living in a material world

What does it profit them if they gain the whole world, but lose or forfeit themselves?

—Luke 9:25

Francis of Assisi is probably one of the most popular and well-known saints. Commonly portrayed as a gentle lover of animals and nature, statues of him can be found adorning gardens around the world. But this is a gross domestication of Francis' real character. Born to wealth and privilege, Francis hungered for more and was initially determined to one day become a nobleman. Instead, he turned away from the comforts of his life and embraced the life of a mendicant itinerant preacher who owned nothing but his clothes and who worked daily for food. Francis never veered from his chosen path and inspired many to follow in his footsteps. Immersed as we are in a consumerist, materialistic society, Francis' choice for radical poverty can seem extreme, but because of this very reality we live in, his example and the spiritual advice he gave his followers has a deeply relevant message we need to hear today more than ever.

early dreams

Francis was born in 1181 (or 1182) in Assisi, Italy, to Pietro da Bernardone, a wealthy cloth merchant (and probably a moneylender as well) and his wife, Pica. From his early youth, the rich, privileged and overindulged Francis was captivated by the chivalric ideal and aspired to become a nobleman either by marriage or by distinguishing himself on the battlefield. Yearning to appear to be what he longed to someday become, Francis cultivated the attitudes proper to a nobleman: He dressed extravagantly, he spoke and treated others with courtesy and gentleness, he gave abundantly to the poor, and he spent extravagantly when he went out on the town with friends, which was often.

While Francis indulged in this lifestyle, trouble began to brew in Assisi. The conflict soon escalated into war with neighboring Perugia. During a battle in 1202 or 1203, Francis was captured along with a number of his compatriots and held as a prisoner of war for a year until his father paid his ransom. The extended captivity took its toll on Francis' health and when he returned home, the twenty-year-old found himself restricted by a long convalescence. Even when he recovered physically, Francis remained somewhat gloomy and depressed.

Finally an opportunity arose for Francis to achieve his longtime dream of becoming a knight through military excellence and he set out in the hopes of making a name for himself. After traveling for a day, he arrived at Spoleto where he stopped for the

We don't know for sure what it was that happened that night at Spoleto to change Francis' mind. One of the stories is that Francis had a dream in which the Lord spoke to him and asked him what it was he thought he was doing and directed him to return to Assisi where he would learn what to do. Another possibility is that Francis learned of the death of Walter of Brienne, whose army he might have been en route to join.

night. There he experienced a change of heart and the next day, instead of continuing on, he turned back for Assisi.

in search of a new path

Although Francis decided not to pursue military glory, it was not immediately clear to him what he should do instead. As he wrestled with determining what direction his life should follow, Francis continued working at his father's shop. Instead of continuing with the carefree life of his earlier years, he focused on deepening his life of prayer and increasing his works of charity, giving generously out of a growing and real care for those in need rather than for the sake of appearances.

As he continued along this path, Francis experienced another transformation through his encounter with the lepers in the area. There were about five leper communities in the vicinity where those stricken with the disease were segregated by law. Francis was just as averse to coming in contact with these outcasts as most of his contemporaries were, until a day came when an experience of grace enabled him to follow Jesus' example of compassionate care for lepers. Francis reflected on that experience with the following words: "...for when I was in sin, it seemed too bitter for me to see lepers. And the Lord himself led me among them and I showed mercy to them. And when I left them, what had seemed bitter to me was turned into sweetness of soul and body."[6]

From that time forward, caring for lepers remained one of his main concerns.

The next significant step that shed light on Francis' path was a vision he experienced before the crucifix in the church of San Damiano. As he prayed on one occasion in this church, he heard Jesus speak to him the words "rebuild my church." The enthusiastic young man took the words literally and

There are many stories about Francis' Edenic connection with animals. It is such stories about wolves, birds, crickets and bees that have transformed Francis into the meek and peaceable statue found in gardens today and into the patron of the environmental movement.

began the process of repairing and rebuilding churches with his own hands and using his father's money to purchase needed materials. Such manual labor was beneath a man of his social standing and evoked his father's outrage: It was not enough that Francis was squandering his money by giving it all away; now he was bringing shame to the family with his crazy behavior.

In an effort to help Francis reconsider his actions, his father locked him in a room in the house. But while he was away on a business trip, Francis' mother tried to reason with him and, failing to do so, set him free. When Pietro returned to discover the treachery, he was furious. Refusing to let the matter go, he sought official reparation for all the money Francis had used for his various projects and brought the issue before the bishop in one of the most famous episodes in Francis' life. Francis arrived at the full church to confront his father and went to the side room. There he disrobed, returning naked with all the clothes and money he still had in his possession in his hands. These he returned to his father while the bishop covered Francis with a robe. Through this encounter Francis turned his back unequivocally on the life and family he had and embraced a new life and family in the church. The encounter also indicated a rejection of money and possessions at a time when entrepreneurs and merchantmen were on the rise in favor of a spiritual path Francis was still discovering.

a new path found

Donning the garments of a hermit, Francis continued his work of restoring churches in the area. He obtained the needed funds and materials by begging, sometimes doing so at the door of former friends. He also asked others who looked on to help him with his project: Some did and others did not. Although the reparation of churches was his main focus, Francis continued to devote himself to prayer and penances, to the care of lepers and other works of charity.

After two years of living in this manner, the twenty-seven-year-old Francis heard a passage from Matthew's Gospel proclaimed at Sunday

Mass that greatly resonated with him—the story of Jesus sending his disciples on a missionary trip with only the bare essentials. After Mass Francis asked the priest to explain the Gospel passage, to make sure he had understood its meaning properly. The priest affirmed Francis' understanding and finally Francis knew what he wanted to do: live the life of a mendicant, itinerant preacher. Losing no time, Francis simplified his garb and set out to live and preach among ordinary people, owning or saving nothing other than his clothing and working daily for food. In Francis' eyes such radical poverty inspired and reflected radical dependence on God as well as complete identification with the poor he felt called to serve.

Here is part of the reading Francis heard proclaimed: "As you go, proclaim the good news, 'The kingdom of heaven has come near.' Cure the sick, raise the dead, cleanse the lepers, cast out demons. You received without payment; give without payment. Take no gold, or silver, or copper in your belts, no bag for your journey, or two tunics, or sandals, or a staff; for laborers deserve their food" (Matthew 10:7–10).

spiritual leader

It wasn't long before Francis attracted his first followers. The small group of companions Francis led shared a commitment to follow and preach the gospel and to live in radical poverty. In addition, Francis sent them on missionary trips with the agreement that all would return annually for a gathering on Pentecost. The reception of their message was mixed: Some people listened and found their words compelling; others weren't sure what to make of them—they seemed either mad or truly holy. Those who were certain they were mad often mistreated them because of it, throwing mud at them, beating them, refusing them hospitality. Regardless of the treatment the companions received, they never retaliated, holding firmly to Francis' teaching that their life of discipleship was characterized by a call to joy and peace.

Once he had gathered a dozen companions, Francis set out with them to Rome to obtain approval for their group. He was cautious that

Francis wrote his famed "Canticle of the Creatures" in praise of creation in the last years of his life. The hymn reveals Francis' sacramental vision of creation, a vision that regards created matter as revealing and giving praise to God, its Creator, by its very existence. Saint Aquinas and Saint Bonaventure would later elucidate and expound this vision in their writings.

they not fall victim to heresy as had happened to other similar groups of the time. He also recognized that in order to fulfill their preaching ministry, they needed ecclesiastical permission and protection. Once he obtained an audience with Pope Innocent III, Francis made his proposal. The proposal didn't meet with immediate endorsement but neither did it meet with disfavor. The pope gave Francis verbal approval for him and his followers to pursue the way of life he had outlined—one of preaching, penance and poverty. Permanent approval would not come until years later in 1223 under Pope Honorius III.

In the next year Francis and his followers settled in the Assisi area on land lent to them by the Benedictines near a small church. The laymen and priests who formed the group had abandoned their possessions and rejected the accumulation of wealth, choosing instead to work daily for their living. In addition to their commitment to poverty, the brothers balanced active times of itinerant preaching among ordinary people with times of retreat from the world.

Many found Francis' lifestyle inspiring and sought to join his growing community. In 1209 a young noblewoman by the name of Clare Offreduccio heard Francis preach and approached him for guidance as to how she could live in a manner that embraced his vision of discipleship. With Francis' help, a monastery was established in poverty at a house next to the Church of San Damiano for Clare and the women who soon joined her (the religious community is now known as the Poor Clares).

Not all those inspired by Francis could abandon their possessions and obligations. But Francis offered advice for them, too, and those who formally chose to follow this path eventually became known as third order Franciscans. Essentially, Francis offered exhortations that reflected his concern to ensure that all of his followers remain faithful to the teachings of the church. He urged those who sought his direction to model themselves after Christ, who humbled himself for our salvation, and to lead Catholic lives—that is, to participate in the celebration of the sacraments, especially through the reception of Eucharist and regular confession and to show respect for church leaders.

Clare, her sisters and her mother, were pious aristocrats devoted to prayer and the care of the poor long before Clare met Francis. When Clare joined Francis, he cut her hair as a symbol of her withdrawal from the world (her hair is still displayed in Assisi).

the growth of the franciscan order

Francis did not limit his preaching to his native Italian land. He had always dreamed of preaching the gospel of peace and truth in the Muslim world and had attempted to do so twice before setting out for the Middle East one final time at age thirty-eight. After a stop in Syria, he arrived at the crusader camp laying siege to the city of Damietta, Egypt. At some point before or after the city was breached, Francis made the daring and dangerous move of crossing the line of battle in order to preach to the caliph and his court. There are disputed stories of trials of fire in the encounter that followed, but what remains undisputed is that Francis was one of the few Christians willing to share his faith in Muslim lands with words rather than with a sword. It is because of this example that Francis' followers were inspired to continue to stand as witnesses in these lands and still have such a strong presence in the Holy Land.

Francis' own pilgrimage to the Holy Land was cut short by the arrival of Brother Stefano, who urged him to return and stop the changes to the community that were being proposed. By this time the community had grown to over three thousand brothers and the sheer numbers demanded organization and planning. Even before Francis' missionary trip, organizational questions had begun to surface, and the community had been struggling to address them in order to ensure the burgeoning movement survived into the future. Upon his return and in the coming years, Francis helped provide the foundational rule that would be approved by the pope. But once approval was gained, he stepped aside as leader, recognizing he may have provided the vision, but he was not the man to enforce it. Instead, Francis chose to trust the order to God while he continued to live the simple life of a brother, a life he hoped would continue to inspire others to remain faithful to their call.

Despite the fact that Francis recognized he was not the one called to lead the organization his vision had birthed, he mourned and struggled to accept the loss of the initial purity of his idea, particularly where poverty was concerned. Francis had preached complete poverty— neither the community nor the individual brothers were to own any possessions. But such radical poverty was untenable for the organization and the brotherhood began to mitigate the observance of poverty, a change that Francis was saddened to see.

letting go

When he was about forty-two, Francis went to a hermitage in Greccio for Christmas. The feast of Christmas—with its focus on the incredible act of humility that was the Incarnation, God becoming one of us—was one of Francis' favorite celebrations. Deciding to recreate the Bethlehem scene, maybe since he had been unable to travel there himself, Francis secured the use of a stable—including the animals—and set the stage for the celebration. When all was ready and the time was at hand, his fellow brothers and people from the vicinity joined him. Moved by the experience, Francis preached with great emotion, as if he were present at the birth of Jesus. The powerful impact on others is evidenced by the fact that a few years later a chapel was built on the site and the custom of celebrating Christmas with a Nativity scene soon became widespread.

Francis probably stayed at the hermitage through Easter before traveling north with his friend Brother Leo to Mount La Verna to fast and pray. Francis probably came to this place of retreat with a heart still struggling with disillusion over what was happening in the order. While praying to accept God's will as Christ had done in Gethsemane, Francis saw a vision of an angel and experienced the stigmata, the imprint of the wounds of Christ on his body. The exact nature of the experience is difficult to ascertain, but the stigmata does reflect Francis' vision of Christ. The humility of the Incarnation that awakened Francis' wonder and devotion was brought to fulfillment in the self-emptying of the cross, a self-emptying Francis had embraced in his life of poverty. Christ crucified was the model of Francis' life, the one he aspired to imitate, and at his time of spiritual trial it does not stretch the imagination to believe it should be a vision of the Crucified that restored Francis' peace and joy.

Having received the consolation he needed, Francis returned to Assisi. He set out on two more preaching missions, hampered by his declining health. Sensing that death was near, Francis asked to be taken to the Portiuncola, the place where he considered his journey to have really begun. During his final days he expressed to the brothers his final wish that he be stripped and placed naked on the ground before burial. The request recalls the scene with his father and suggests Francis saw his death as the final leaving behind of this life while being embraced by a new one. Francis died during the

The claim that Francis had received the stigmata was the first such claim. The stigmata would not be included in the declaration of Francis' canonization, and although its historicity would be defended and later accepted by the church, the church would never claim divine intervention was involved.

Two years after Francis' death, Pope Gregory IX celebrated his canonization in the city of Perugia, and his remains were transferred on May 25, 1230, to the lower church of the basilica that was being built in Assisi. They still lie there today.

night of October 3, 1226, when he was forty-five, and was buried at his home parish of San Giorgio.

REFLECTION
a material world

We live in a consumer society. We all say it, we all talk about it, we all know it, and we're all part of it. On a daily basis we are bombarded by advertisements for the latest gadgets and gizmos we must have to be happy, flaunt our economic status and get what we want out of life. We're told that money makes the world go round, and the more of it we have, the better off we will be. Assailed as we are by these messages, they do sink in to a lesser or greater degree. We don't all necessarily become heartless capitalists engaged in the blind pursuit of wealth, but most of us come to like the stuff out there, to enjoy having it and to getting more of it.

In light of this, Francis' choice to give up his wealth and material possessions for a life of hardship and poverty seems pretty out there. His desire to live in radical dependence on God might be admirable, but the need to do so by rejecting all material goods seems unnecessarily radical and difficult to fathom, especially today when embracing the practices of fasting and abstinence seem archaic and passé even among those who practice their faith. What is so wrong with wanting and getting the good things in life—the fabulous vacation, the designer clothes, the car with all the bells and whistles, the monster TV? We work hard for them. Why shouldn't we enjoy them and get as much of them as we want?

inside the material world

Nothing is wrong with things in themselves. Nothing is wrong with wanting stuff. Nothing is wrong with getting stuff. Until, that is, something is wrong with us. It doesn't happen all of a sudden, few of us notice it is happening at all, but, given the consumer nature of our society, it is difficult to avoid it. Our natural hunger for more becomes narrowly defined in material and physical terms—the myth that money and objects will fulfill our desire and lead us to happiness. Some of us recoil at hearing that claim, certain we don't buy in to this myth because we are not truly materialistic. Yet the focus of our careers becomes earning more money, money with which we will one day be able to afford a McMansion in that posh neighborhood, money with which we can spend without worrying about collectors, money with which we will retire in luxury. We put up with a job we hate, working with people we dislike, all for a good, maybe even fat, paycheck.

Unconsciously, without our noticing, we start to live our lives as if they were one big, all-consuming competition for the pot of gold at the end of the rainbow, a competition in which someone else's gain means there's less for me, a competition in which every person I meet is a potential opponent. Without giving much thought to it, we come to approach everyone and every situation with self-centered thoughts: Can this person help me, or is she standing in my way? What am I going to get out of this situation? How can I get him to implement my idea? We even treat God this way, complaining that we don't "get" anything out of Mass, or that God doesn't listen to us when we don't get what we want. Not only do we unwittingly treat everyone as a means to our end, we start to approach every relationship in an adversarial, businesslike manner, measuring what we must give to get what we want, keeping score of everything said and done, storing ammunition to ensure we are always the winners.

Too busy striving for the dream of striking it rich or working hard to keep the dream attained, few of us take a moment to stop and look at the person we are becoming in the process. If we did, we would see that even with the money and stuff we are not happy; rather, we feel a profound emptiness and dissatisfaction when we allow ourselves to feel anything at all. When we look at our relationships, we realize no one really knows us, and we don't really know anyone else; doing so would mean letting someone else see our weaknesses, and weaknesses in a competitive environment can be used against us. When we stop to look at ourselves and what we've become, we realize we've been holding on so tightly to what we have that the fear of losing it has been keeping us from opening ourselves to any new gifts and possibilities that might come our way.

the path to a new vision

As Francis began his journey of letting go of the wealth and position into which he was born, he began to experience an interior transformation that deepened and grew, as did his embrace of poverty. The more Francis let go of his material possessions, the greater was his compassion for others, his ability to appreciate the created world, his own joy and desire to help others find and follow the true path that leads to it.

When asked for guidance on this path by those who could not embrace poverty as he did, Francis shared advice that even today can help us avoid the pitfalls of consumerism. The heart of his path as presented to the average person was celebration of the sacraments. This answer might seem formulaic to us today and irrelevant to the question of money, materialism and consumerism. But embracing a truly sacramental life can have everything to do with helping us overcome the negative effects of the sometimes toxic culture we live in, for it is a path that helps us see people and things in a new and richer way.

The celebration of the sacraments is about recognizing the divine light in the people and the stuff of the world in the context of a supportive community. When we truly begin to live our lives sacramentally, we begin the slow process of discovering the light of God at work in us and in our environment. Carrying this vision into our daily lives can help awaken in us the recognition of the inalienable dignity of those with whom we interact and of all things in creation, calling us to treat them with reverence and respect. Living through this sacramental lens invites us to recognize that we are not in competition with each other or the world, but rather, are deeply connected in the Spirit of God, and as such our fates are intertwined, rising and falling together.

As we begin to walk this sacramental path, we experience the same transformation Francis did, a transformation that makes us more compassionate, more caring, more human. Rather than approaching everyone and everything as a means to our ends, we begin to see others in his or her own right. Rather than approach every situation as a win-lose competition, we begin to approach them as opportunities where we can all benefit. Rather than living in fear of losing what we have, we live with the freedom of knowing what we have cannot be taken away. Rather than living in a distant future, we start to truly enjoy and appreciate the present we realize we are blessed to have.

Like many of Francis' contemporaries, we may not all be able to embrace poverty or may simply not be ready for such a radical step. But his advice still offers us the insight that can help us become more Christ-like in a society that needs us to be so.

REFLECTION QUESTIONS

How would you feel if you lost all your money and material possessions? What would you do? How would you feel if you had an overabundance of them? What would you do?

What role do money and material possessions play in your life? How do your pursuit of them and your efforts to hold on to them influence your decisions and your relationships with people?

Have you ever fallen into one of the traps of materialism and treated people as a means to an end? Have you ever approached life as a competition or thought of things or people only in relationship to your own needs and wants or related to people as your enemies?

In what ways do you already live your life sacramentally? How can you continue to cultivate and deepen this approach and open yourself up to its fruits?

four

CATHERINE OF SIENA

discovering the truth

The light shines in the darkness, and the darkness did not over-come it.

—John 1:5

Catherine of Siena is one of those saints who inspires awe—at her courage and daring, at her dedication and zeal, at the combination of her involvement in mundane, ecclesiastical and political affairs of her time and at the miracles that flowed from her. After spending her childhood and adolescence mainly devoted to a quiet life of prayer, penance and fasting, Catherine discerned that God was calling her to service out in the world. The service that began with her family gradually grew and expanded, leading this woman whose very presence inspired a profound and lasting conversion on those who met her to counsel all people and mediate in all disputes. Throughout her industrious years Catherine never abandoned the spiritual practices that led her to discern this call and continued to sustain her in her work in the face of continuous gossip and suspicion. Catherine's commitment to a rich spiritual life despite the busy schedule she maintained challenges any of us who claim to be too busy with other important responsibilities to cultivate our own spiritual lives.

the beginning of the journey inward

Catherine was born in Siena—the twenty-fourth of twenty-five children—to Monna Lapa and Giacomo Benincasa, on March 25, 1347. Giacomo was a quiet, hardworking and virtuous man who supported his family though a prosperous wool-dying business; Monna was anything but quiet and a force to be reckoned with, but both shared strong religious values which they instilled in their children.

When Catherine was only six years old, she had her first significant religious experience. As she and her brother Stefano walked by the Church of Saint Dominic on their way back from visiting their sister Bonaventura, Catherine looked up and saw before her Christ the King with Saints Peter, Paul and John. Transfixed by the sight, she remained frozen in place while her brother continued walking, unaware she wasn't following. Realizing his mistake, Stefano returned and pulled her to move her along. When he did so, Catherine awoke from her contemplation and her vision vanished. Catherine burst into tears. From that moment on, Catherine firmly set her mind on the spiritual quest for sanctity. She felt a passion for prayer, but was constantly prevented from finding solitude by her everyday chores and errands. As a solution, she often asked permission to visit her sister, using the long, solitary walks as an escape. She also began to practice penances and discipline, beginning an ascetic way of life she continued throughout her days.

Young though she was, Catherine knew she was called to follow a different path and at the age of seven made a vow of virginity, dedicating herself to Christ in the tradition of the holy virgins. By the time Catherine was fifteen, Monna was exasperated by her disinterest in marriage and enlisted the help of a relative to talk some sense into her daughter. When Father Tommaso della Fonte (her foster brother who had become a priest and later her confessor) spoke with Catherine about her future, she confessed to him her single-hearted desire to devote herself to the Lord and her certainty that she was not called to marry. Father della Fonte suggested to Catherine an action through which she could show her family she was serious about her vocation: To her family's horror, she cut off her hair, which effectively cut her off from society. Her family felt insulted by her action and punished her by removing all her privileges, hoping to impede her long periods of prayer and penance and redirect her interests.

Catherine embraced her punishment. Denied the privacy of her own room, she cultivated an interior sanctuary for prayer and meditation that could never be taken away. Forced to serve her family as a kitchen servant, she looked upon them as the holy family and her service to them as service to Christ. Finally one day Catherine announced she had taken a vow of virginity and that nothing would change her mind, for she was certain this was God's will for her. Realizing Catherine's actions were not part of a passing interest, Giacomo restored her to her rightful place in the family and, with her family's consent and support, Catherine continued pursuing her chosen path.

the culmination of the journey inward

The next significant moment in her spiritual journey was brought about as a result of the onset of chicken pox. Fearing for Catherine's life, Monna was willing to do anything. All Catherine asked was that she be allowed to become a Dominican tertiary, a religious order whose championing of truth greatly appealed to her. At Monna's request, the prioress of the Sisters of Penance agreed to send a few sisters to interview Catherine with the understanding that if the interview went well, she would be accepted. The sisters who met with Catherine returned impressed with her spiritual maturity and she was accepted in the order upon her recovery.

For the following three years, the sixteen-year-old turned her complete attention inward, practicing strict silence and leaving her

Dominican tertiaries (or third order Dominicans) were not enclosed religious. Rather, they were elderly women or widows who lived in their own homes, practiced charitable works, and gathered for prayer and spiritual exercises. A non-enclosed order was unusual enough; an unmarried girl of Catherine's age pursuing a religious vocation in this non-enclosed way was unheard of.

room only to attend Mass on a daily basis. These three years were an intense period of purification during which she was assailed and tortured by visions and temptations of evil. In the face of temptation, Catherine was perplexed by the apparent absence of the God who had consoled her so graciously all her life. Despite her feelings, she prayed constantly, expressing her trust in the Lord despite the doubt that troubled her.

The turmoil ended as suddenly as it began when Catherine realized that dedicating herself to God meant accepting "the bitter as sweet." With this simple realization the demonic visions that had haunted her lost their power to frighten her and she felt closer to God than before. In this renewed closeness, she asked God where he had been while all this was happening to her. To her question God replied by pointing out that God had been with her of course, for if God hadn't, instead of being mortified and repulsed by the evil thoughts that assailed her, she would have found them truly appealing.

During the years of internal reflection, Catherine gained key spiritual insights she shared with her followers. A few of those include the recognition that suffering is temporary and can serve a purifying role in directing the soul toward God as well as the axiom, "You are she who is not; whereas I am He who is." This axiom helped Catherine see herself clearly and honestly as she stood before God. It also reflected the path of true freedom, the path of self-emptying in imitation of the self-emptying of Christ.

Catherine's internal transformation soon started manifesting itself externally in startling ways. After receiving Communion, Catherine began experiencing ecstasies that sometimes lasted for hours and during which she was completely oblivious to her surroundings. These experiences became so disruptive to others that a restriction was set on how often Catherine could receive Communion and, when she fell into ecstasy, she was sometimes physically carried outside the church and left out on the road, a spectacle to passersby.

This period of purification and strengthening culminated with Catherine's mystical union with Christ when she was nineteen. During Mardi Gras, while the citizens of Siena feasted in anticipation of the forty-day fast, Catherine prayed in her room for stronger faith. In response, the Lord appeared before her, accompanied by Mary, John the Evangelist, Paul and King David. While David played the harp, Catherine celebrated her espousal to Christ, receiving a ring only she could see as a symbol of this union.

the beginning of the journey outward

After this climactic experience Catherine began to sense that her time of silence and retreat was at an end. Although she would never stop dedicating hours of her day to quiet prayer and reflection, after three years of hardly interacting with others, she began a new phase of action and involvement in the world. Feeling called to see and love Christ in others, Catherine walked down to the kitchen as the family sat for the meal and began to serve them. Soon she extended her service beyond the confines of her home, assisting the poor and visiting and caring for the sick and leaving behind her a path of deeply transformed lives.

Catherine's gaze, filled with such interest and understanding directed toward the other, is said to have been the inspiration of the conversion of hundreds who met her in person over the years. Such was the power of Catherine's presence and gaze that several priests were always in her company ready to hear the confession of the crowds who were moved to repentance by their encounter with her.

As she continued her work, her fame began to grow. Catherine became a much sought-after mediator in every kind of dispute—within families, between families and eventually between political and church leaders—healing divisions with her compassion and understanding. As word of her skill spread, she traveled farther than what was considered appropriate for an unmarried young woman of the time, sharing her message of reform, reconciliation and conversion with the people of neighboring cities. But Catherine did not limit her reach to those she met. She corresponded with all types of people who sought her wisdom and insight—ordinary citizens, cardinals, civil leaders, even the pope. Her letters carried the same message she preached, urging recipients to greater holiness as the means to achieve a much needed church renewal. In addition, to church leaders she emphasized the need to lead with integrity and along the path of peace, rather than with violence, intrigue and corruption; to ordinary citizens she emphasized the importance of obedience to church leaders, especially the pope, even though their conduct was less than virtuous.

In the course of her life, many became followers of Catherine. This joyful and united group came to be known as *Caterinati* (children of Catherine) and included men and women of all sorts— young, old, married, widowed, religious, lay, criminals, scholars, the rich, members of the nobility, even Catherine's mother became one of her daughter's followers. They referred to Catherine as "mother" and she referred to them as "beautiful brigade" or "our group."

During these years of service, Catherine received several divine gifts that helped her carry out her ministry. In response to her generous and gracious acts of charity to a beggar, a pilgrim and a sick woman who thanked Catherine's kindness with malice, the Lord gave Catherine a jeweled cross, a mantle to protect her from every change in season, and the gift of perceiving the virtue or vice of a soul through her sense of smell—virtue radiated fragrant perfume, vice radiated an unbearable stench, such that she asked people who came to see her to cleanse their conscience before conversing with her. In response to her prayer "for a clean heart," the Lord appeared before her, removed her own heart and replaced it with his

own. Finally, she experienced the partial stigmata on her hand, receiving it fully when she was twenty-eight. It was a gift that at her request
was visible only to herself, and whose pain she was only able to bear
through God's continuous grace.

Catherine's radical dependence on God continued to deepen. She
had practiced fasting and had restricted her diet for many years, but
when she was twenty-five, her passionate love of Christ truly became
the sustaining force of her life. From that time forward she was unable
to keep any food down except for the Eucharist. Though she tried to
hide this development, it soon became public knowledge. The sensation
caused by her inability to eat was only compounded by her desire for
frequent reception of Communion—a practice frowned upon at the
time—and her continued propensity to fall into ecstasy upon receiving
Communion.

Throughout her life reaction to
her work and divine favor were mixed.
Some became her followers, others her
critics, and, as her fame grew, so did
gossip about her. Although Catherine
dismissed and ignored what was said
about her, church leaders could not
long ignore the scandal Catherine's
extremism was causing. In June of 1374
Catherine was asked to travel to
Florence for a formal investigation
conducted by the master general of the
Dominican Order. The investigation
cleared Catherine from suspicion
(although the gossip never died) and the order indicated the degree of
approval and recognition of her authority by assigning a distinguished
member of the order as her spiritual director, the man who would
become a dear friend and her biographer, Father Raymond of Capua.

Several of those counted among
the *Caterinati* have been
declared blessed in the Catholic
church:

- Blessed Raymond of Capua
- Blessed Stefano Maconi
- Blessed Guglielmo Flete
- Blessed Tommaso Caffarini
- Blessed Giovanni delle Celle
- Blessed Giovanni Opizzenghi
- Blessed Giovanni di Gabriele
  Piccolomini
- Blessed Chiara Gambacorti
- Blessed Bartolomeo Serafini

the culmination of the journey outward

Despite Catherine's tireless preaching and writing urging reform at all levels, the situation in the church and society continued to worsen. When a terrible dispute arose between Florence and papal representatives, Catherine was asked to serve as an ambassador to the Italian city-state before Pope Gregory VII, who was residing in the French city of Avignon. Unable to resolve this particular matter, Catherine still managed to impress the pope so greatly that she ultimately persuaded him to return to his see in Rome. The pope may have been timid about the move, which was sure to encounter opposition, but Catherine was convinced he could initiate the needed church reform only from Rome. In January 1377 Pope Gregory VII entered the city of Rome, ending the seventy-year Avignon exile.

The pope's return inspired a spiritual rebirth that ended too soon when an even greater calamity befell the church and all of Europe. Overburdened by the task before him, Pope Gregory died the year after his return. The turbulent events surrounding the ensuing papal election combined with the next pope's initial conduct (Urban VI) precipitated the election of another pope, Clement VII, and the beginning of a forty-year schism. The schism marked one of the darkest times in the

When Catherine returned to Siena after the conclusion of the investigation, it was to a city suffering from an outbreak of the plague. Despite the danger of contagion, Catherine stayed with her followers and worked in the hospital caring for those who had fallen ill. Her courageous and selfless work won Catherine much praise in the neighboring city of Pisa, leading to an invitation from its citizens to come and share her message with them.

Ironically, it was in the midst of these darkest of times that Catherine wrote her seminal work, *The Dialogue*. It is a discourse between Catherine and God in which she shares all the key spiritual insights she had discerned throughout her life, a work of true genius given that she never took a theology class and didn't even learn how to write until she was twenty.

church and had a divisive ripple effect throughout every level of a European society forced to decide which pope they would follow.

Despite growing evidence of Urban's mental instability, Catherine supported him as rightful pope and worked tirelessly to bring about an end to the schism. She demonstrated such great courage throughout these dark times that even the pope commented that she put the rest of them to shame. But Catherine's efforts, courage and determination were not enough to end the bitter division. Taking to heart the devastation that assailed the church, Catherine became gravely ill in January 1380 and suffered painfully for several months until her death on Sunday, April 29, at the age of thirty-three. It would be thirty-seven more years before the schism was ended during the Council of Constance in 1417.

Catherine was canonized by Pope Pius II in 1461 and declared a doctor of the church on October 4, 1970, by Pope Paul VI. Her feast day is celebrated on April 29, and she is the patron saint of nurses, the sick, and those suffering from temptation or ridiculed for their faith. Her remains are enshrined in the Dominican church in Siena and beneath the high altar of St. Maria Sopra Minerva Church where Catherine was first buried.

REFLECTION
discovering the truth about ourselves

Although a member of a large and noisy household, Catherine spent most of the early years of her life in relative seclusion. As a young child she avidly nurtured her relationship with God during her quiet, solitary walks to visit her sister and the time she devoted to prayer and penances in the privacy of her room. When these were no longer possible, she continued an internal retreat until her family permitted her to pursue her heart's desire, and she returned to the quiet confinement of her sparsely furnished room to continue her time of prayer, reflection, fasting and penance, combined with the regular participation in the celebration of the Mass.

This quiet and reclusive existence is the complete opposite of our busy, fast-paced contemporary lives. During all that time spent alone with no phone, TV, iPod, not even books or games, did she not get bored or lonely? If we heard about someone living such a life today, we would probably think this person was depressed, had agoraphobia or at the very least was antisocial. Far from being symptomatic of psychosocial problems, Catherine's time of retreat was a time of discovery and confrontation facilitated by her chosen spiritual practices. During these years of intense internal activity, Catherine's knowledge of and relationship with God deepened and strengthened while her understanding of the mystery of sin, the power of temptation, the truth about who she was before God and the nature of the human person increased exponentially.

Today, we talk a good talk about self-knowledge and there are plenty of self-help books out there to aid us. But if truth be told, most of us are unwilling to do as Catherine did and truly face the demons that hide in the darkness of our own hearts. Most of us are content with a cursory look inward that yields the profound statement: "I'm OK. I'm not doing the terrible things those other people are doing." But self-examination and prayer as Catherine practiced should yield so much more: It should enlighten us as to why we act as we do, open our eyes to our passions, our weaknesses, our strengths, to what annoys us, troubles us, tempts us, but most importantly to the need for God in our lives.

discovering the truth about our call

The fruit of Catherine's time of retreat was not only increased wisdom. Eventually, Catherine's life of prayer led her to discern a call to serve out in the world. For someone who was not naturally outgoing and who lived at a time when unmarried women didn't move freely about society, this was a call that challenged her to step beyond what was comfortable and accepted. As she began to respond to this call, she did so by serving those immediately around her—her family, the sick at the local hospitals, the beggars in the streets she walked. As she continued to respond to this call, her outreach expanded beyond the city limits and her service also evolved and grew, increasing her impact on the world. Despite her increased activity, Catherine never stopped devoting time to prayer, never stopped the spiritual practices that had given birth to this mission and continued to sustain it throughout.

For those of us who question the need for taking time for quiet reflection and prayer when there is so much to be done, Catherine's life says to us that without such retreat we will never discover our purpose in life, our call. Many of us long for a meaningful life, long to make a difference in the world, to have such a purpose. Many of us feel at bay, pushed and shoved haphazardly by the constant demands on our time, energy and effort, yet are unable to stop this circuitous dance because we lack an alternate direction in which to channel our energy. When we reach such a state, we cannot afford *not* to take the time for prayer and reflection, to take the time to cultivate our spiritual life.

As we begin to discover our path, the one God is beckoning us to, like Catherine we must respond with openness to the possibility that God might call us to step out of our comfort zones and do something that doesn't come naturally or that isn't really done in modern times and might raise some eyebrows even in our "enlightened" society. As we continue on the path we have discovered, like Catherine we will find that our call deepens, expands, matures. As we continue on this path, like Catherine we must never abandon the spiritual practices that gave birth to our mission, for it is this spiritual life that will sustain us through the joys and the challenges, the successes and the failures that we are sure to face.

discovering the truth about our purpose

Although Catherine's ministry met with much success, even this great saint was not immune to failure, and even though her ministry had such a positive impact on so many, there were those who still regarded her and her work with suspicion, derision and doubt. Risking failure, risking being fodder to the rumor mill, risking bearing the brunt of smear campaigns—none of these is what most of us are jumping up and down to sign up for. When we sign up, we're hoping for the moments when we get to see how our work has transformed another person's life, the moments when we see real change happening right in front of us, knowing we had something to do with it. The false accusations, the doors closed, the cases lost; when they first happen it can come as a shock to realize that responding to God's call doesn't wrap us up with protective gear against failure and opposition.

Faced with failure or suspicion, we cannot forget that Catherine's sustaining force remained her relationship with God, which she nurtured throughout her life with continued reception of the Eucharist and the quiet time she devoted to prayer. Without this solid foundation, she could have easily succumbed to self-doubt fueled by the whisperings of others. It was the peaceful center in her heart that reaffirmed her in the path she had discerned, which sustained her with the confidence and courage to persevere despite the obstacles before her. When we face opposition or seemingly insurmountable challenges as we respond to God's call in our lives, like Catherine, we will only be able to move forward if we remain rooted in the spiritual life that nurtured the discovery.

Difficult as it is to bear failure and opposition, heartbreaking as it can be to see much of our devoted time, energy, passion and life crumble tragically before us, ultimately the purpose of our lives as Catherine reveals to us is not the visible manifestation of our accomplishments we all hunger to see. The purpose of our lives is to turn our hearts to God, to respond to God's deepening call as we discern it in the context of our relationship with God regardless of what the world might say or do in response. The way we turn our hearts to God, the exact balance we strike between the time of action and the time of prayer, the spiritual practices we draw from to guide and sustain us on this path will probably not look the same as Catherine's, but they should lead us to the same discoveries and ultimately the same destination.

REFLECTION QUESTIONS

What are your spiritual practices? Do you devote time to self-reflection? To individual and communal prayer? Do you have a spiritual director or mentor to help you as you seek to grow in your relationship with God?

What kind of action is God calling you to? How have you been responding? What strengthens you to persevere?

What challenges or risks do you fear facing? What challenges have you faced in the past? Who supports you on your path? Who feeds your self-doubt?

five

TERESA OF AVILA

aspiring to spiritual greatness

For nothing will be impossible with God.

—Luke 1:37

From the time she was a child, Teresa was captivated by the idea of heaven. As she matured, so did her understanding of this hope and of the kind of relationship with God it expresses. Despite an early experience of union with God in prayer, Teresa was not yet ready to turn away from the carefree life she enjoyed, so she spent many years in what she later regarded as spiritual mediocrity. All this changed when an encounter with the crucifix brought her face to face with her shortcomings and she received the grace to overcome them and embrace the course of spiritual greatness that lay before her. With a changed heart, Teresa devoted what remained of her life to prayer and the work her prayer inspired her to pursue, mainly initiating a reform of her religious order and writing extensively on the spiritual life. For those of us whose spiritual lives are on cruise control, Teresa challenges us to aspire to rise above the comfortable steadiness in which we languish and respond wholeheartedly to God's unconditional love for us.

childhood and youth

Teresa Sanchez de Cepeda y Ahumada was born to Don Alonso Sanchez y Cepeda and Doña Beatriz de Ahumada in Castile, Spain, on March 28, 1515. A precocious child, energetic, impulsive, beautiful and eager to please, Teresa was much loved—her father's favorite.

From early Christianity, martyrs and hermits were highly regarded due to the sacrifice they embraced. The martyr shed his or her blood for the faith in imitation of Jesus' sacrifice. The hermit lived in solitude striving for the salvation of souls through prayer and penance.

From a young age Teresa developed a strong concern for her eternal destiny. The idea that the joy of heaven or the pain of hell would last forever captivated her religious imagination. She fixated on this truth with the tenacity and grit that would serve her so well later in life, and she came up with various schemes to ensure she would go straight to heaven. First she convinced her older brother Rodrigo to venture with her to a territory in southern Spain occupied by the Moors, where she was confident they would be martyred—and martyrdom, she knew, guaranteed direct entry to heaven. Alas, her plan was foiled— apparently due to the fact that she had caring parents! One can imagine how crushed she must have been to find her wonderful vision ruined by her interfering parents! But Teresa was not one to give up easily, and she soon came up with an alternate plan: to create a hermitage for herself. Once again Rodrigo was recruited as her partner in crime. Once again the plan was foiled. This time the logistics worked against them: Rodrigo and Teresa just couldn't seem to build a hermitage that wouldn't crumble around them. With this second unsuccessful attempt, Teresa gave up her schemes for the time being, but her concern for her eternal destiny would recur later in her life.

Having abandoned her plans for immediate passage to heaven, Teresa turned her attention to the everyday affairs that filled a young girl's day, becoming a typical teenager. She loved romance stories, nice clothes, perfume, jewelry, talking and gossiping and was very concerned about what others thought of her. In addition, Teresa claims to have been very clever about hiding from her father any indication that she was less than a perfectly well-behaved young girl—a typical teenager indeed!

Her carefree days ended when her father sent her as a boarder to an Augustinian convent. The sixteen-year-old Teresa was not at all interested in becoming a nun and was not too happy with her situation. But she accepted it, suspecting even her craftiness had not been enough to hide the increasing frivolity of her life from her father, and soon she found contentment in her new home. Teresa came to admire the nuns and to feel less reluctant about taking the habit herself. In fact, as her thoughts became once again concerned with her eternal destiny, she began to seriously consider this possibility.

the choice for religious life

In Teresa's time women only had two options in life: Enter a convent or get married. When Teresa weighed her two choices, her primary consideration was determining which path was most likely to get her to where she wanted to go: heaven. On one hand, she did not really believe she had a true vocation to the religious life. But in her day this was not an impediment to entering a convent. On the other hand, Teresa was not convinced marriage was all that desirable for reasons she didn't specify—maybe it was seeing her mother age prematurely in a good marriage, fear of dying in childbirth, or maybe she disliked the thought of the restrictive life it would entail.

Teresa agonized over her two choices until she made herself ill and had to be sent home before reaching a decision. On the way she stopped to visit with her uncle Don Pedro. While there he asked her to read to him. His reading choices were of a much more spiritual and enriching nature than anything Teresa would have picked, and they had a very positive effect on the distressed young woman. As she read, Teresa found the words caused her thoughts to become concerned with spiritual matters and the ultimate destiny of her soul. Reconnected to the path she had begun to pursue as a child, Teresa decided that the safest course of action was to become a nun. Once decided, Teresa demonstrated the same unwavering determination she had exhibited as a child and would not back down before her father's initial opposition, leaving home secretly one early morning in November to enter the Convent of the Incarnation. She was twenty-one.

Once in her new home, Teresa knew she had made the right choice. Later in life Teresa would look back on these early happy times as God's reward for having conformed herself to God's will.

first conversion

The year after she made her final vows, Teresa grew very ill. The doctors were at a loss. Deeply concerned, Teresa's father moved her to the mountains to be treated by a healer. On the way there, Teresa stopped once again at Don Pedro's. During her stay Teresa read a book on the life of prayer that changed her life. In *Third Spiritual Alphabet* Francisco de Osuna spoke of prayer as intimacy with God, a view that resonated with Teresa's own hunger and that she would develop in her own later writings on the life of prayer. Osuna also introduced Teresa to a form of prayer known as interior recollection (a form of mental prayer). The prayer of interior recollection Osuna presented described a path of prayer that led one to turn one's senses inward and leave everything else behind in a journey to meet God at one's center. Teresa became an avid follower and her interior life flourished as she practiced this form of prayer.

While her interior life grew, her physical health declined until she fell into a cataleptic state—essentially paralyzed and seeming to all to be dead. Fortunately her time was not to end yet. A few days later Teresa opened her eyes to find them heavy with wax (in preparation for her burial) and to learn that a tomb had been prepared for her. Alive but completely paralyzed, weak and in great pain, she was brought back to the convent. It took a long eight months for her to recover her strength and return to her normal level of activity. During her convalescence Teresa continued her practice of prayer of recollection that awakened a perceptible holiness that touched and moved those who saw her.

Unfortunately, once her health returned, so did Teresa's less than virtuous inclinations. She abandoned the prayer of recollection that had led her to such spiritual growth and her prayer life became one of rote, plagued by her struggle with distractions and aridity. Of her struggles in prayer, she writes:

By the sixteenth century the rule of the Carmelite Order had been considerably mitigated—that is, made significantly less rigorous. The rule of enclosure, for instance, was fairly lax. The nuns were allowed many and regular visitors, and they were encouraged to spend long periods of time away from the convent and stay with relatives to help manage costs. There were also significant differences in the lifestyle of the nuns: Those with wealthier families, such as Teresa, enjoyed many luxuries while those from poorer families led a much harder life.

> ...very often, over a period of several years, I was more occupied in wishing my hour of prayer were over, and in listening whenever the clock struck, than in thinking of things that were good. Again and again I would rather have done any severe penance that might have been given me than practise recollection as a preliminary to prayer.... [W]henever I entered the oratory I used to feel so depressed that I had to summon up all my courage to make myself pray at all.[7]

Despite living in a convent, she turned again to the social whirl, chatter and gossip of visits from friends and relatives she had always enjoyed. This social activity was not the worst evil, but Teresa was aware it was not the life God was calling her to live and her conscience plagued her, never convinced by the litany of excuses others accepted to explain why she had abandoned the prayer of recollection.

second conversion

Teresa's life continued in this vein for almost twenty years. Finally one day during Lent she had a transforming experience of grace. When the thirty-nine-year-old nun entered the chapel and came face to face with the image of Christ, she was struck by the contrast between her own mediocre response to God's love and that of Christ's. Heartbroken, she threw herself to the ground, expressing the determination not to rise until God promised to strengthen her in her resolve to change. Experiencing the reassurance of a new resolve in her heart, Teresa rose, convinced God had granted her request.

Armed with renewed strength, Teresa's prayer life began to deepen and change. In the years to come she would share her insights on prayer in her various writings. She describes prayer as a journey inward to meet our most intimate friend, the One who created us and loves us unconditionally. The journey requires increasing detachment from the concerns and entanglements of the world, a letting go that opens the pray-er to receive and be open to God's love and vision. At the beginning stage the pray-er is doing most of the work, but, as the pray-er progresses, God does more and more of the work until finally God is doing it all. And the fruit of the life of prayer, as Teresa's own life attests, is growth in love of God and of neighbor.

As her prayer life changed, Teresa's life was transformed. In her autobiography Teresa reflects on this transformation: "Until now the life I was describing was my own; but the life I have been living since I began to expound these matters concerning prayer is the life which God has been living in me—or so it has seemed to me."[8] Her earlier struggle to let go of frivolous friendships, relationships and pleasures ended after a mystical experience in prayer. From then on she evaluated relationships on the basis of whether or not the other person shared her love of God and her desire to do God's will—high standards for friendship indeed!

mystical experiences

During this time of deepening prayer, Teresa had begun to experience mystical visions. When she first began experiencing them, Teresa was concerned. While praying she felt an inward assurance these visions were a divine gift. But later she would grow fearful they might be the work of the devil. Unable to discern with certainty the source of her

prayer experiences, she sought direction from a priest with a local reputation for holiness. After listening to the details of the graces Teresa had been receiving in prayer, Father Daza concluded they were the work of evil spirits and recommended she seek further guidance from one of the Jesuits who had come to the area. Deeply troubled, Teresa prepared to do as advised.

Father Juan de Pradanos, a Jesuit who came to see Teresa, told her otherwise. He encouraged her to continue her prayers, believing that she was being led by God and that God might be using her to help others. This greatly consoled Teresa.

Teresa followed Father Pradanos's advice and continued her path of prayer. The mystical visions returned, offering Teresa comfort and strength. Despite the positive judgment from

During her visions, Teresa sometimes "heard" God's voice. At other times she "saw" Christ, the Virgin Mary, angels and the souls of a few people she had known. She describes the experience made famous by Bernini's statue as follows "In his [the angel's] hands I saw a long golden spear and at the end of the iron tip I seemed to see a point of fire. With this he seemed to pierce my heart several times so that it penetrated to my entrails. When he drew it out, I thought he was drawing them out with it and he left me completely afire with a great love for God. The pain was so sharp that it made me utter several moans; and so excessive was the sweetness caused me by this intense pain that one can never wish to lose it, nor will one's soul be content with anything less than God."[9]

the Jesuits regarding her visions, others continued to regard them with suspicion. Teresa had to defend and explain her gift against repeated accusations that her visions were demonic in nature, fabricated or the fruit of her own delusion.

renewal begins

The importance of Teresa's visions lay not only in what they revealed about God, but the greater love they engendered in her, a love she put into fierce action. A few years after the beginning of her visions, Teresa had a conversation with a few other sisters and laywomen regarding their desire to establish a convent that followed the primitive rule more closely. Soon after, Teresa experienced a vision in which God revealed to her that such a convent would indeed be established, that its name would be Saint Joseph's and that it would serve him well.

Teresa's view of cloistered life was not the grim, gray life some of us might imagine. Yes, the sisters were to lead a life of strict enclosure, contributing to the good of the church through a life of contemplative prayer, but Teresa's guidelines for her sisters call for a joyful life, and once the convent was established, passersby could sometimes see them dancing and singing inside.

With this mandate and conviction, Teresa began the long and arduous process of establishing this new convent. Teresa's intent was to establish a small convent in poverty for thirteen nuns at the most. This would mean that the town would have to support it through charitable donations, a move that raised much opposition. Furthermore, women entering the convent would leave their worldly identity at the door, not even bringing a dowry to assist with the financial support of the convent. Despite the strong opposition and temporary setbacks, Teresa was confident the outcome would be as God had revealed. Once Teresa finished the tiring work of renovating the house, four nuns moved in. Saint Joseph's was finally established and eventually accepted, and with it was established the Reformed Carmelite Order, the Discalced ("shoeless") Order.

But Teresa's trials and Herculean efforts were only at their beginning. Four years later Teresa began searching for a location for her second convent, and more would follow as she embarked on the renewal of the Carmelite Order. By the time of her death she had established sixteen reformed convents. She worked at an amazing pace given the many challenges she faced: poor health, terrible travel conditions, violent opposition and unpopularity, being denounced to the Inquisition, attempts to suppress the reform, lawsuits and the ever-present suspicion about her visions that spurred rumors and gossip about her. But Teresa was undaunted by all these challenges. Her perseverance and good humor through all these trials is astounding to say the least and give witness to her unfailing faith in God.

It was soon after making what proved to be her last foundation that Teresa fell gravely ill. After making her last confession and expressing her peace of mind and heart in the face of death, she passed away on October 4, 1582, at the age of sixty-seven.

Teresa was beatified in 1614 by Pope Paul V, and canonized in 1622 by Pope Gregory XV. On September 27, 1970, Pope Paul VI declared her and Catherine of Siena doctors of the church, the first women so named. Teresa of Avila's feast day is October 15 and she is the patroness of Spain, bodily ills and headaches and people ridiculed for their faith.

REFLECTION
a goal worthy of pursuit

Some of the most difficult questions to answer in an interview are any that force us to imagine ourselves in the future, to share a glimpse of our ambition, our dreams or hopes for the future, the direction in which we envision our life heading. Aside from the difficulty of trying to answer the question in a way that will get us the desired outcome is the challenge of committing ourselves, even for a moment, to a particular path and simultaneously closing other possible doors. Even if these doors are only open in our imagination, many of us like to keep them as possible escape routes should we become too frustrated with our current situation. It is true that these short-, mid- or long-range goals and plans can change and remain in flux, but unless we intend to drift through life we need an overarching plan to help us prioritize the demands on our time and energy and sort out when it is time to change direction and when it is time to commit to it.

Teresa had such a life plan since she was a child: She wanted to go to heaven. She didn't pursue this goal single-mindedly her whole life, but it was the goal she would come back to and which would persist in the back of her mind until she *was* ready to pursue it with such dedication. Setting heaven as a goal can seem a rather impractical and ethereal life plan, one only the super devout, the Teresas of this world, would set for themselves; the rest of us live in the real world where we are drowning in work, have bills to pay, people to take care of, chores to finish and some semblance of a social life to maintain—what does heaven have to do with any of that?

Heaven is eternal union with God and being in heaven is being in perfect union with the God who created us and loves us with abandon. Developing and maintaining this relationship as the center of our lives is what this overarching plan is about, and looking at Teresa's life can help us see that it can have very practical and real effects on us and on our lives. From the time Teresa experienced herself strengthened by God to respond wholeheartedly to God's love for her, she was a changed person. It wasn't just that she was experiencing mystical visions; her vision of every aspect of her life shifted as she saw each facet in a new light. As a consequence, she reevaluated her relationships, she reexamined the way she was living out her religious vocation, and she opened herself to new, previously unimagined challenges. Setting our hearts and minds on God has radically practical implications for our lives, but we will only see this for ourselves if we too can embrace this goal.

our achilles' heel

Before Teresa was able to fully embrace a close relationship with God, she spent many years leading an ordinary existence. It wasn't that the life she was leading was a bad one, it was just that it was shorter and smaller than what God asked. Teresa knew she was called to more, but life was too enjoyable and comfortable as it was—she liked being the center of attention and was simply not ready to give it up.

We may not all crave to be the center of attention, but we all have that Achilles' heel that has us ensnared in our comfortable life, unable and unwilling to risk letting go while trying to reach for something more, especially something as intangible as a close relationship with God. Like Teresa, it's probably nothing that would come close to landing us in jail—we finally got that break we worked so hard to get and nothing is going to sidetrack us now; we are at the top of our game and having the time of our life and are going to enjoy it while it lasts; or maybe we finally have our life the way we want it and are not ready to entertain the thought of change or anything that might bring it about. Besides, we are not entirely convinced of the importance or urgency of aspiring to greater spiritual heights: We're pretty good as we are—we're honest, caring, giving, thoughtful and we *do* pray; isn't this good enough?

When Teresa came face to face with the crucifix during Lent of 1554, she realized that "good enough" wasn't good enough when we stand before a God who loves us so much that he became one of us, suffered, died and rose to new life so we could always be with him. Yes, we're OK people, but we owe our all to the God who gave God's all for us. *We* would never accept the kind of constant mediocrity we expect God to accept in our spiritual lives when it comes to our work, our other relationships, even the products we purchase. At the very least we demand that some kind of visible effort go into trying to see that all these attain the highest possible quality. Yet when it comes to our spiritual lives, we coast on cruise control for decades, barely stopping for gas along the way and consider such minimal effort good enough.

change is possible

Stepping on the brakes, pulling out the map, redrawing our route is an immense challenge and the inertia of our path is a strong force to counteract. The first step, as Teresa shows us, is to desire to grow in our relationship with God with both mind and heart. Sounds doable, but of course it's not as easy as it sounds. Intellectually we might want to walk this path, but our hearts have their own agenda and continue to be drawn to the things in our lives we love so much, undermining our resolution. When we are so divided, it is easy to give up and be satisfied with being "good enough." Only if we keep our goal in sight do we have a chance of reaching it, and even if all we seem to do is look at it from a distance, it is better than forgetting about it; for all we know, today might be the day we suddenly find the courage to take a step forward.

After she took that step forward, Teresa discovered the benefit of good spiritual directors and of friendships with people who shared her love of God, of people who supported and strengthened her on her journey. When growing in our relationship with God is already such a challenge, a first step forward can mean seeking a good spiritual director or mentor to help us keep going, or seeking the support of those friends to whom we can open our hearts.

Once we too take that step forward, we will also discover the truth of Teresa's wisdom on the life of prayer: God walks it with us, helping us more and more along the way, enabling us to master the weakness that led to our defeat before. In our own journey we may never experience the mystical visions Teresa did, but we *will* experience the same kind of internal transformation that will positively affect every aspect of our lives. Which brings us back to the initial question: Do we really want to try?

REFLECTION QUESTIONS

Where is your life heading right now? What are your priorities—the ones you want to be your priorities and the ones that are really your priorities? What is your overarching life plan that gives direction to everything else?

After examining your life, what would you say is your Achilles' heel? How does it shape and influence your life? How might your life be different if it played a smaller role?

How do you ensure perseverance in striving toward a closer relationship with God? Who supports and guides you on this journey?

six

ALOYSIUS GONZAGA

shaping our character

Or do you not know that your body is a temple of the Holy Spirit within you, which you have from God, and that you are not your own?

—1 Corinthians 6:19

Aspiring to holiness from a young age, Aloysius Gonzaga pursued a life of purity with the single-minded focus others devote to the pursuit of Olympic gold. He resisted the social pressures of his day to lead the life of a courtier by cultivating a deep spiritual life and keeping his focus on living in the manner to which God called him. Eventually discerning a call to the religious life, he resisted his father's pressure to give up the idea, finally winning him over instead. Having fulfilled his vocation, he died at the early age of twenty-three, with no regrets, ready to respond to God's final call. Like Aloysius, we all experience pressure from various fronts to act in certain ways, to live up to certain expectations. In the face of such pressure, Aloysius offers an inspiring example that it is possible to resist conforming ourselves to the dictates of others when these dictates run counter to our becoming the people we know God calls us to be.

his father's son

Aloysius was born on March 9, 1568, in Castiglione, in the region of Lombardy, Italy, to Donna Marta and Ferrante Gonzaga. The Gonzagas were of a princely family, and as the firstborn Aloysius was heir to the territories his father governed. His birth was followed by that of a brother, Rodolfo, and then seven more children.

As the boys grew up, Ferrante became concerned that Aloysius was too soft. Military man that he was, Ferrante decided to take the four-year-old heir with him while he trained his troops, hoping to shape him in a manner more suited to his destiny. At the camp Ferrante outfitted his son with a complete suit of armor (made to size of course), lance, sword and even a small pouch with gunpowder. Aloysius did not disappoint, mastering the soldier's skills as his father had hoped. Unfortunately, he also mastered the soldiers' colorful language, unaware of its profanity, let alone how inappropriate it was for a boy of his social position. When Ferrante went abroad and sent Aloysius back home, his tutor addressed this issue with him and Aloysius corrected his language, realizing soon enough what he had been saying.

Giving Aloysius a pouch with gunpowder turned out not to be the best idea. He was an excellent pupil and once he had learned how to load the gunpowder into a weapon, he apparently tried it one night with no supervision, narrowly avoiding injury and causing such a commotion his father thought a mutiny was afoot. Upon discovering it was only his son, he dispensed punishment that included no more access to gunpowder, trying to hide his pleasure at seeing such a display of daring.

When his father returned from his military duties, he was happy to find Aloysius maturing into a self-possessed, determined young man. He had hoped his son might grow up to be a military man, but now he saw that his son exhibited qualities that would allow him to pursue a greater path, the path of a statesman. What Ferrante didn't know was that his son was also cultivating other qualities, spiritual qualities that were awakening a desire to pursue a religious vocation. Aloysius prayed daily the penitential psalms, the prayers called the "Daily Exercise" and the Little Office of Our Lady, initially reciting them until he later learned meditation and extended his prayers to incorporate this practice as well.

embarking on a new course

In order to polish and complete their education, Ferrante sent his two eldest sons to Florence under the tutelage of the Grand-Duke Francesco de Medici. At court Aloysius was expected to devote his time to his studies and to the social activities of his class and age group. Boredom was the number-one malady affecting courtiers and all sorts of games were planned and played to pass the time. These games ranged from the inane to the shameless and shocking—the sixteenth-century version of spin-the-bottle and rainbow parties. But Aloysius was determined to keep himself pure and to avoid serious sin. Immersed in a society where purity seemed impossible, he grew to loathe court life and all the trappings of his wealth and social status. He began to withdraw from those social events and situations where he might be expected to be in close proximity to women and temptation, not caring that people began calling him a "woman-hater."

With more time on his hands, Aloysius began to deepen his spiritual life. He went to confession more frequently and spent more time in prayer. He decided to make a full confession of his life, which helped him see what he might have become had he continued down the path of his early childhood and to recognize the danger of thoughtlessly going with the flow and following one's tendencies.

One of the practices he adopted to protect his eyes from possible temptation and keep his vision pure was keeping them cast down. It is ironic that one of the reasons he was able to do this without getting lost in the city for not minding where he was going was that the entourage of servants that went with the princely young man ensured he arrived at the proper destination.

Finally, he made a promise before Our Lady to keep himself pure in body and spirit. He didn't just want to avoid sin, but he wanted to become holy and always serve God. Despite the fact that he was only ten, Aloysius was not the type to make promises lightly, and he firmly intended to keep this promise. Given his self-control and determination, there was a good chance he would do just that.

The practice of the discipline was not unusual in his day, strange though it may strike us today. Aloysius saw firsthand the extreme corruption and degeneracy of his age, and although he did not believe he could make up for it himself, in a way, he saw his own practice of the opposite virtues of purity and self-control as a way of contributing to the expiation of the sins of his time.

Aloysius began to intentionally set himself on a path that would help him achieve his goal of purity. In addition to his current spiritual practices, he began reading the lives of the saints and contemplating the possibility of becoming a priest and handing over his inheritance to Rodolfo. When he developed strangury and had to go on a restrictive diet, he found the forced fasting helped him enter into and gain a deeper understanding of the suffering of Christ, and he embraced it as a permanent spiritual practice. Later he also embraced the practice of spiritual discipline, also in part because it helped him identify with the sufferings of Christ. Finally, he began serving at Mass, and, after receiving his First Communion, began receiving Communion weekly (an uncommon practice at the time).

staying the course

Aloysius' resolve to serve God was tested when the entire family accompanied the Empress Mary of Austria and her retinue to Madrid, Spain, in 1581 where the fourteen-year-old Aloysius served as page of the first class to Don Diego, the prince and heir of the Spanish principality of Asturias, Spain. Court life in Spain was somewhat different from the Italian courts Aloysius was used to, in part because of the cultural differences, but boredom was still the great enemy. Duty-bound to participate in various activities, Aloysius began to feel his resolve to remain pure eroding.

Sensing this danger, he found a regular confessor and continued to reflect on his vocation, growing certain that it lay in joining a religious community. After much thought Aloysius started leaning toward joining the relatively new Society of Jesus. He found the order's combination of contemplation and action, its focus on education and missionary work and its vow of poverty all very appealing. But what settled his interest was the order's rejection of ecclesiastical honors. To Aloysius, this meant that if he became a Jesuit, even if his family wanted to heap honors upon him as a way to increase the family's prestige, he would be unable to accept them, and he desperately wanted to leave behind the trappings of his family's position.

facing his father

Having intellectually come to a decision, Aloysius sought confirmation from God. While in prayer he experienced such a confirmation through that quiet voice in his heart he knew to be God's. Sure of his path, he shared his decision with his confessor, who counseled him to obtain his father's permission before proceeding further.

For all Aloysius' iron will and determination, he did not relish the thought of telling his father about his plans. So he took the back door and asked his mother to test the waters for him. Upon hearing the news, Ferrante exploded in fury, lashing out at Marta, at Aloysius and at his confessor. When he calmed down, he began to suspect this was all a ploy to get him to stop the gambling problem from which he had been suffering, and it took his cousin's intervention (the General of the Franciscan Order) to convince Ferrante that Aloysius was sincere about his plans to enter the Jesuit order.

While Ferrante was still reeling from the shock of hearing his son's plans, Don Diego died of smallpox. In Aloysius' mind, this meant his duties in court were at an end and he was free to assume other duties of his choosing. When he and Rodolfo (and their servants) went for a walk in the city and took a detour to the Jesuit college, Aloysius went in and told his brother and servants to leave without him. Ferrante immediately sent someone to fetch Aloysius with the message that if he was going to take this step, rather than causing such embarrassment for the family in the process, he should at least come home and proceed in a dignified manner and leave from his own home. Reassured of his father's consent, if not support, Aloysius returned and they all left for Italy in 1584.

the battle of wills

Despite his reassurance, Ferrante was far from ready to abandon his hope that Aloysius would one day become a great statesman. He played all the cards he could think of to persuade his son to abandon the course of his choice: He sent him with Rodolfo on a grand tour of Europe. Aloysius gritted his teeth, so to speak, and went, refusing to wear the new clothing made for the occasion or to abandon the path of purity he was on. Ferrante brought everyone he could think of to talk some sense into Aloysius, to at least persuade him to become a secular priest rather than a Jesuit. But none of these efforts swayed Aloysius.

It was Ferrante who began to give way. The initial break in the ice occurred when he went to Aloysius' room to investigate the reports he had heard of his son's severe disciplines. He probably went with the intention of rebuking his son, but instead, the evidence of his son's self-scourging moved him and he gave him permission to move forward with his plans.

When he arrived at the novitiate at Saint Andrea, Aloysius was embarrassed to discover that despite his belief that he was giving up his privileged position and coming with only a few things, he had brought four times as many belongings as the average novice. Once he had settled in to the novitiate, it didn't take long for his fellow novices to discover the same exceptional qualities Ferrante had seen in his son and, convinced he would one day become general of the order, nickname him "Generalino" or "young general."

Before Aloysius could enter the novitiate, he had to legally renounce his inheritance. While he waited for the process to run its course, he agreed to go to Milan to conduct business on his father's behalf. While Aloysius was in Milan, Ferrante had a change of heart and again tried to persuade his son to abandon his path. Frustrated, Aloysius returned home. Discord between them continued until finally Aloysius told his father he was in his hands, but warned him that refusing to let him go would be going against God's wishes. Ferrante broke down and cried, recognizing the battle was lost.

unexpected challenge

Meanwhile, the legalities of Aloysius' abdication were complete and the seventeen-year-old was free to enter the Society of Jesus. As many young men do, Aloysius found the novitiate a somewhat frustrating experience: He was asked to fast less, do less penance, spend less time in prayer and that his time was not his own. He alternated between feeling he had done a good thing and feeling despondent and uncertain that he possessed the qualities needed for such a vocation. But amidst his periodic doubt, Aloysius was confident that with God's help he could become what was needed and he threw himself into the enterprise with zeal and dedication.

As a novice, Aloysius served at Masses, studied and visited prisons and hospitals, despite the fact that the sight of blood made him faint. To give himself courage to get through these visits to the sick, Aloysius would imagine the sick man was Christ and that Our Lady was placing him in his care. He also began going out to the marketplace to teach Christian doctrine, something he had done back home for the local children. A crowd would gather to listen, and ultimately the group would make its way to

Not long after he consented to Aloysius' decision, Ferrante came to truly believe Aloysius had been right after all, a belief that led to a profound conversion in him. Ferrante made a full confession, abandoned his gambling and followed a more faithful practice of prayer, dying a happy man in 1586.

the college with Aloysius who had persuaded them all to make their confessions!

While tending to the needs of others, Aloysius did not forget to continue his own self-examination. His confessor at the time was Robert Bellarmine, who descibed Aloysius as one of those rare individuals who could look at himself with honesty, had a very clear grasp of his gifts and shortcomings and didn't waste time wishing to be what he wasn't or trying to control what he couldn't.

the clash of the old and the new

The final test of Aloysius' resolve to leave behind the wealth and position he had been born into arrived in the shape of a family feud that threatened to lead to war at worst and murder at best. Rodolfo, who had inherited Ferrante's holdings, was locked in a land dispute with the duke of Mantua. The emperor had ruled in Rodolfo's favor, but the judgment had not been accepted. Knowing Aloysius had the necessary character and skills to settle and enforce a decision, the Empress Eleanor of Austria and Donna Marta wrote to the Jesuit general requesting Aloysius' intervention. Aloysius' superiors agreed that he should go.

Aloysius spent the next several months on this diplomatic mission, traveling back and forth between Castiglione, Brescia and Mantua, visiting his brother and the various people Rodolfo had angered. While working on a peaceful resolution to the conflict, Aloysius found himself fighting another battle as well: Back in the heart of Gonzaga land, people greeted him and treated him not as the religious he now was, but as the Gonzaga prince he had been. Refusing to fall back into the life

Aloysius had hoped that by joining the Jesuits he would be freed from the weight of the Gonzaga name. He soon discovered he had yet to complete this break. He was easily identifiable as a Gonzaga, and people stared and made comments, particularly given his shabby attire. During the course of his studies he was required to participate in disputations and presentations, and when he did so, was often embarrassed to find one or more Gonzaga cardinals (and their respective entourages) in attendance.

he had intentionally left behind, Aloysius had to constantly put his foot down and demand others remember and respect his new identity. By the time he returned to Rome, he had succeeded on both fronts: He had persuaded the duke to accept the emperor's decision and he had done so while maintaining his integrity.

final call

As he journeyed back to Rome, the seeds of another bout of plague were sown: Severe famine, the forerunner of disease, was setting in and by 1591 the plague had reached Rome. The Society of Jesus had served victims of the plague when it had struck before, and the order tended to the needs of the sick once again. At first Aloysius contributed to the mission by raising funds, but soon he asked for permission to help in the hospital. Concerned about the threat of contagion, his superiors hesitated before they agreed to his request.

Aloysius' aversion to hospitals hadn't vanished, yet he forced himself to tend the afflicted, carrying them to their beds, washing and feeding them, despite the repugnance these tasks awakened in him. With a growing number of young Jesuits falling prey to the plague, Aloysius' superiors finally forbade him from returning to the hospital. At Aloysius' insistence he was permitted to continue his work in the non-contagious wing.

But God was calling to Aloysius, who sensed he did not have long to live. He came back sick from one of his hospital visits, and lived in a weakened state for another three months until his death on June 21, 1591. In the face of death Aloysius was not afraid, nor was he disappointed it would claim him so young. As much as he wished to continue serving the sick, he felt he had done what God had wanted him to do and he had no unfinished business or unachieved dreams left to pursue.

Aloysius' relics are entombed under the altar in the church of Saint Ignatius in Rome. He was beatified in 1621 by Pope Gregory XV and canonized on December 13, 1726, by Pope Benedict XIII. He is the patron saint of teenagers, AIDS patients and caregivers.

REFLECTION
shaping who we are

From a young age Aloysius had been exposed to foul language. Not knowing better, he simply adopted what he heard as we all know children are prone to do. He had the good fortune of being taken in hand by his tutor, who pointed out to him how inappropriate his language was, and Aloysius changed. Later in life when Aloysius reflected on this moment and saw where the path of continued use of such language could have taken him, he shuddered at having been spared this fate.

It doesn't sound so terrible of course—what's a little swearing in the grand scheme of things? But Aloysius had the vision to recognize a truth many of us happily ignore for much of our life: Our words, our thoughts, our hearts and our actions are all connected, and when one is in the mud, the others will soon follow. When Aloysius examined himself, he didn't just see foul language; he saw what the next step would be.

We all find ourselves exposed to all sorts of behaviors, yet we believe we've outgrown the childish sponge-like tendency to take in and repeat what we're exposed to. But if we are honest, we can all recognize that we still incorporate some, if not a lot, of the behavior of the people and culture that surround us: other people's patterns of speech, the corporate way of doing things, the style of dress, what we purchase, what books we read, what music we listen to. None of this is necessarily bad, but the only way for us to realize if any of it is bad is to stop and reflect on who all these things are turning us into and to consider whether that is the person we hope to become and, more importantly, that God calls us to be.

purity

At first Aloysius' hope of who he would become was simply someone who never committed a mortal sin. Soon that hope was transformed into the more positive hope that became his path to holiness: He hoped he would remain pure, as befitting one who belonged to God. When

Aloysius said *pure,* he wasn't just talking about sex, although it did include that. Purity to Aloysius was bigger. Purity was about what he said, what he saw, what he heard and what activities he took part in— basically every sphere of his life.

This may sound like a lack of appreciation for or even rejection of life and all the wonder it has to offer, but Aloysius didn't deny that creation is good, that life is good. He simply kept his eyes focused on the ultimate good in the shadow of which other pleasures become transient and unimportant. And keeping his eyes focused as he did, he saw himself first and foremost in terms of his relationship with God, of who he was before God, rather than in terms of who he was in the world, and shaped his life accordingly.

In thinking about who we hope to become, many of us at some point develop plans and dreams that, if accomplished, will make us great. In doing so, we look at our lives from the world's perspective first, forgetting that in God's eyes we already are great. We are children of God, unconditionally loved by God, and there is nothing greater we can become, all we need is to see and accept this truth and act in a manner that reflects it. Embracing purity is a way for us to allow the holiness of God to flow outward from our hearts, to touch every aspect of our lives and the lives of those around us, and in this way help us become the holy children of God we are created to be.

getting there

Aloysius didn't magically become a virtuous young man. Aloysius exercised the same kind of focused discipline in pursuing his goal as an Olympic athlete. Keeping in mind the path he was called to follow, Aloysius continually resisted the pressures of his family and society to live the life of privilege and decadence he was expected to and which was handed to him. He accepted that he was susceptible to temptation and took great care not to place himself in potentially "bad" situations or to remove himself quickly from them when he couldn't avoid them. He prayed regularly, maintaining a strong relationship with God, the source of his strength and inspiration, and he examined his conscience and confessed his sins regularly, recognizing and admitting his failures.

Such self-discipline can seem unattainable to us—like achieving Olympic gold. Yet it's not a question of how much self-discipline we've exhibited in the past, but about the strength of our faith in the vision that motivates us, our trust that God will help us become the people God created us to be. It is this strength that can propel us to take the first step—maybe a word or action, a thought or reflection—and to take the next one. Soon we will begin to feel ourselves changing, becoming different people—kinder, more compassionate, more self-aware, more understanding. And maybe most importantly we will begin to feel happier with who we are as we start to realize that maybe there was something to this purity thing after all.

REFLECTION QUESTIONS

What does the passage from 1 Corinthians 6:19, "Or do you not know that your body is a temple of the Holy Spirit within you, which you have from God, and that you are not your own?" mean to you? What does it say to you about God? What does it say to you about who you are?

When you take an honest look at yourself, the way you treat yourself and others, the way you speak, the way you dress, who do you see yourself becoming? Is this who you want to be? Is this the person you believe God is calling you to be? If not, what would you like to change about yourself? What steps would you have to take to begin making that change happen?

How do you incorporate time for reflection on your life, the direction in which it is headed, and what influences and shapes it? Who helps you engage in such reflection? Do you keep a journal, celebrate the sacrament of reconciliation, or practice any other spiritual discipline that helps you stay on track?

seven

MARTIN DE PORRES

responding to our neighbor
in need

*Then the righteous will answer him, "Lord, when was it that we
saw you hungry and gave you food, or thirsty and gave you something to drink? And when was it that we saw you a stranger and
welcomed you, or naked and gave you clothing? And when was it
that we saw you sick or in prison and visited you?" And the king
will answer them, "Truly I tell you, just as you did it to one of the
least of these who are members of my family, you did it to me."*
—Matthew 25:37–40

Martin de Porres is a much-loved saint from Peru. Admired for his
holiness and generous care of the sick and poor since his youth, this
wonderful man was a miracle of industry, eager to share and give witness to God's love through his daily labor and charitable work.
Nothing could stop this deeply compassionate man from responding
joyfully and patiently to the daily needs of hundreds in the convent
where he lived and in the wider city of Lima. Despite his many years of
service, he never stopped treating each person with reverence and

respect, nor did he become disheartened at seeing that the need never went away. Challenged as we are by a different variety of the same social problems, Martin's lifelong dedication to helping the person before him with unwavering faith and care continues to offer valuable guidance and insight to those of us struggling to respond to our neighbors in need today.

the beginning of charity

Martin de Porres was born on December 9, 1579, in Lima, Peru, the illegitimate son of Don Juan de Porres, a Spanish nobleman, and Anna Velazquez, a free black woman. When Don Juan looked upon his son, instead of pride and joy, he felt disappointment. With his dark features Martin took after his mother, and Don Juan refused to acknowledge him and Martin's younger sister, Joan, for eight years. This initial rejection led the young Martin to seek and find comfort in God the Father, and the adult Martin to show special concern for the plight of orphans and abandoned children of the city.

Martin's path to holiness began early in life. As a child his mother would give him money to go to the market to purchase food for the family. But the way to the market was filled with people in desperate need. Despite his mother's repeated efforts to try to impress upon him that they were in need of food too, Martin couldn't deny help to anyone and often returned empty-handed. Martin would never outgrow or lose to cynicism this generous and selfless response to the needs of others. On the contrary, his compassion grew as his relationship with God deepened.

Other Saints of Lima from the same time period:
- Saint Turibius de Mongrovejo
- Saint Francis Solano
- Saint Rose of Lima
- Saint John Massias

Martin's trips to the market did more than provide an opportunity for him to practice charity. When he ventured out, it was also his habit to stop at every church along the way to say a prayer to his heavenly Father. These prayerful stops signified only the initial steps in his life of prayer.

Through the years Martin continued to nurture his desire to grow closer to God, a desire that we can surmise from events in his life that eventually blossomed into a mystical union with God.

The foundations of compassion and prayer were evident early in Martin's life, but his third great gift emerged through his father's intervention. After seeing to Martin's and Joan's early education, Don Juan provided enough money to ensure he learned a trade. Martin chose to be trained as a barber, which in those days was a combination of barber, pharmacist, doctor and surgeon. Under the tutelage of Marcel de Rivero, Martin learned his trade quickly and displayed an unusual level of natural aptitude.

Martin regarded his medical practice as his ministry to the sick and poor and refused to accept payment for his services. If any money was given with insistence, Martin used it to help those in need. Yet even as his workload increased, Martin did not neglect his spiritual life and adjusted his schedule to make time for both God and others. He continued visiting churches, but did so early in the morning, before work. And after a full day's labor, he spent time at home praying and doing spiritual reading.

Lay helpers or "*donados* were members of the Third Order who offered their services to a monastery and lived there permanently, receiving food and lodging as compensation for their work. They took upon themselves the heaviest tasks and were considered as ranking below the lay brothers. Their habit was a white tunic and a black cape, but without the scapular and capuce."[10]

the beginning of religious life

Martin hadn't been engaged in his trade very long before he began to feel in his heart that what he was doing was not enough. His reflection led him to seek entry to the Dominican convent of the Holy Rosary. His decision came as an unwelcome surprise to his clientele. Despite his youth Martin was known throughout the city for his skill and holiness, and the general sentiment was that it would be a waste for such a gifted and exemplary young man to retire from the world. But Martin had grown certain he was called to give himself fully to God and that the convent offered the path through which he could achieve this union. At the age of fifteen he was accepted in the Dominican convent as a lay helper, the humblest of posts.

When news about Martin's decision reached Don Juan, he also raised objections. He didn't oppose his son's entry into the convent, but his pride was wounded to find he had done so in the lowest of positions. If Martin entered a convent, the least he could do was take vows as a brother. But Martin felt very strongly that being a lay helper was suitable and appropriate for him and he would not be swayed. Probably recognizing his own stubbornness in his son, Don Juan gave up. As things turned out, eight years later members of the order invited Martin to take vows—which meant changing the rule that denied this option to blacks and mulattos—and this time Martin gladly accepted.

Even before professing vows, Martin lived according to the Benedictine rule and spirituality of sharing the fruits of contemplation with the world through actions. Martin was always very busy with his manual and domestic chores, but while he worked, he cultivated a contemplative mode of prayer. His prayer was not limited to contemplation during the day. At night he followed Saint Dominic's example of practicing the discipline three times during the night: the first time to enter into union with the sufferings of Jesus, the second time as reparation on behalf of sinners and the third time for the souls of purgatory. Martin also practiced regular fasting by rarely, if ever, eating meat, and when he slept—which was not very often—he never did so on a comfortable bed.

Martin's love for God's creatures also included animals. At his sister's house he cared for unwanted animals and is said to have persuaded the mice that infested the convent to settle instead in the back garden where he would provide them with food.

the fruits of prayer

As Martin's prayer deepened, his union with God seems to have become as complete as one could hope for in this lifetime. While in prayer before the cross, Martin was known to levitate to the height of the crucifix, arms extended in the shape of a cross. Indeed, on one occasion a group of religious saw a light coming from the altar. When they approached for a closer look, they saw that the light was focused on Martin, who was lost in prayerful ecstasy.

But the fruits of Martin's contemplation extended far beyond levitation and ecstasy. His medical skill was probably already known to those in the convent, and it was not long before Martin's duties were increased to include responsibility for the infirmary. This meant that in addition to the servile tasks he already performed and did not relinquish, he cut the hair of the three hundred or so religious, plus tended the sick among the religious, the slaves and servants who worked on the land that belonged to the convent, and those of the neighboring Dominican convent. At one point when the city was struck by an epidemic of measles, sixty of the religious were ill and under his care. Through the ordeal, Martin tended to each one, never showing revulsion or impatience, never giving the appearance of being rushed or too busy to offer comforting words, clean sheets or a cool drink. His care of the sick did not end with this respectful and comforting treatment. Martin had a gift for knowing how an illness would progress and knowing when the end was sure and near. In fact, frequent

Locked doors were never a barrier for Martin when he was on a mission of service, and when necessary this gift extended to those with him. Once, Martin had taken a group of novices for a walk. As they walked, Martin spoke of spiritual matters, losing all sense of time. Unfortunately, this meant they would all be late coming back. Martin felt responsible, and simply encouraged the novices to take heart and trust in God. Soon the novices found themselves back in the convent, just in time to join the religious for communal prayer. How they got there so fast, how they came in the locked door, none of them could explain.

visits from Martin during a serious illness usually meant one's death was approaching; infrequent visits meant one would mend.

But sometimes when natural remedies did not work and nothing more could be done, Martin would pretend to try one more thing to hide the truth of his miraculous touch. Martin would never admit to what he had made possible, nor would he stick around to take any credit, and never would he think about boasting. What he did was "simply" pray with the confidence that God, in God's goodness, would bring healing where Martin had failed—and God would answer his prayer. One such instance occurred when Francisco Velasco, a novice, fell very sick with dropsy. Doctor Cineto, the physician who treated him, pronounced that nothing more could be done and gave the young man only a few more days to live. Not only was poor Francisco at death's door because of his dropsy, he was kept in strict isolation to prevent him from reaching for water and precipitating his own death. During the night Martin came to see him. He quietly washed him, changed him and remade the bed with clean, dry sheets. Francisco finally asked Martin whether he was going to die. In turn Martin asked him if he wanted to die. "No!" Francisco declared. In that case, he wouldn't, was Martin's answer. Francisco relaxed, calmed down and was finally able to sleep through the night. In four days, he had recovered enough to move around on his own. Doctor Cineto was astonished and declared it a miracle.

the expansion of charity

Martin's love of neighbor not only poured itself forth in his care of the sick, but he also had a burning desire to share his own love of God with others. On a regular basis his superiors sent him to Limatambo, a nearby property owned by the order. During the day Martin tended to his duties. Once he had finished, rather than relax, he spent the time caring for the sick among the slaves and servants, extending his care to health education and evangelization, and eventually, spiritual counseling. He spoke about God with passion, and his own example of charity and compassion was living proof that he believed what he spoke. Many were moved by Martin's words and example to seek baptism, for it was as true then as it is now that there is no more persuasive evangelizer than a living witness.

It was not just unbelievers in whom Martin awakened a deeper love of God. Novices whose perseverance was floundering found their faith restored and revitalized by Martin's passionate words about the vocation to the religious life.

But Martin longed to carry the torch of faith beyond the confines of Peru and be a missionary in foreign lands. Despite the fact that he never left Peru, God granted Martin his heart's desire. Lima saw the arrival of many travelers; included among these was a man on his first trip to the city. Not long after his arrival, he met Martin, only it wasn't their first meet-

There are many stories indicating Martin had the gift of bilocation (being in two places at the same time). On one occasion he went to visit his sister and her family, who were out of the city, to help restore peace among them, yet did not miss any of his duties at the convent. On another occasion a merchant from Lima fell ill while in Mexico and called out for Martin, who came and ministered to him. When he had fully recovered, the man went to the Dominican convent in the city to thank him only to discover Martin had never come to Mexico.

ing. The new arrival instantly recognized Martin—how could he forget the man who had sustained his faith and that of his companions during their incarceration in Africa and raised the needed amount of gold to set them free? As usual, in his sincere humility, Martin refused to accept the words of gratitude or try to explain how he had been able to accomplish such a task.

As a child, Martin had never been able to deny assistance to those in need; as an adult, he not only responded to the needs of others, but he also displayed a God-given ability to discern the needs of those who didn't voice them. From the doors of the convent, Martin distributed

Martin's gift of knowledge extended beyond discerning the needs of his patients and the poor. Despite never having taken any courses in theology, Martin was known to have settled theological arguments by quoting Thomas Aquinas's *Summa*, even providing the references. He also knew where to find "lost" or "misplaced" items, and when someone was "borrowing" money or supplies he had set aside for the needy.

food and goods to those who came in need of them before going out in to the city to distribute more, sometimes showing up with exactly what was needed without having to be asked. If he came upon someone who was sick and homeless, he carried them to the convent for treatment until his sister provided a place he used as a type of clinic. He had a running list of at least 165 families whose needs he regularly provided for. In addition, on a daily basis he traveled five miles to bring necessities to soldiers stationed in the area.

addressing social problems

One of Martin's deepest concerns was the children of the city. The Spanish conquest had left a vast number of orphans and lost, unwanted or abandoned children in need who suffered from hunger and were easily preyed upon and taken advantage of. The problem was so monumental it was deemed unsolvable. But Martin couldn't turn a blind eye to what he saw and he prayed for guidance and direction as to what could be done. His prayers were answered and he saw a way to address the problem by raising awareness that the situation was unacceptable and by tapping into the public's conscience. Soon Martin had the support of the archbishop and the viceroy and sufficient funds to open an orphanage and school for street children, the Colegio de la Santa Cruz.

There was another problem that drew Martin's attention: the number of women without an adequate dowry to either enter a convent or get married. A lack of dowry meant a very precarious situation in a society with few options for women. A local man named Don Mateo Pastor had provided the bulk of the money needed for the school, and at Martin's request he agreed to provide the enormous sum needed for dowries for each of the seventy-seven young women Martin had identified. Although the underlying social problem persisted, for these women Martin's action was a much-needed lifeline.

Martin tirelessly continued his charitable work for the remainder of his life until his peaceful death in the convent where he'd lived for forty-five years on November 3, 1639, after a brief period of painful convalescence.

Martin was beatified in 1837 by Pope Gregory XVI and canonized on May 6, 1962, by Pope John XXIII. He is the patron saint of African Americans, biracial people, barbers, hairdressers and stylists, racial harmony, social justice, Peru, public education and public schools. His relics are housed at the reliquary at Santo Domingo Church in Lima along with the relics of Saint Rose of Lima and Saint John Massias.

REFLECTION
whom do we see?

Most of us have probably had the experience of walking along a city street and hearing the rattle of coins in a cup combined with the sight of a homeless person sitting or standing on the sidewalk and asking us for some spare change. The words of others seem to come unbidden to our mind: "If you give them money, they'll just spend it on drugs or alcohol; better give the money to an organization." Sometimes we listen to those words—partly because we believe them, partly because we're on our way somewhere and don't really want to stop and dig around for change. Other times, before we can walk by, our consciences raise unwelcome objections: "How do *you* know what they'll spend the money on? And who are you to judge them if they do spend it on drugs and alcohol? And are you really going to set aside the money you wouldn't give to this man now and give it to a charitable organization?" And just like that we're not just faced by one homeless person asking for money, but by the entire problem of homelessness and how to address it and think about it and suddenly, it seems easier to find a smile or some change and move on.

There were many beggars in Lima in Martin's time. And it must have been just as true then as it is now that giving them money, food or clothes didn't solve the problem of homelessness or poverty. But Martin never thought to just walk by and ignore a person in need, he was never troubled by the fact that the same people continued to need help for years, and he wasn't blind to the fact that some of them tried to take advantage when they could. He was probably just as aware as the rest of us that some of the people he helped were unsavory characters, but if he came across them, he helped them anyway. Not only did Martin help them, witnesses who knew him state he did so with reverence and respect, always careful not to cause embarrassment or draw attention to the person's need. For when Martin walked by a person in need he didn't just see a beggar, but Martin saw the face of Christ in the neighbor in need before him and could never just walk away.

the example we follow

For some of us what holds us back from responding with generosity and care is fear. We fear that if we give of ourselves too freely, we'll be taken advantage of and have the life sucked out of us. It is a fear promoted by society's message of looking out for number one. There is certain truth behind this cautious attitude. There *are* people who will take from us and take as much as possible when there is something to be taken. There *are* people who will try to manipulate us when we try to help them. There are even, as Martin's life attests, people who will literally steal from the hand that helps them. So to protect ourselves from being taken, we walk around with blinders on, helping those in need from a safe distance.

But as Christians, we are called to follow the example of Jesus who held nothing back, who gave it all for us. Martin followed Jesus' example with each act of charity and kindness. All his life Martin gave with generosity, joy and humility, without judgment, condemnation or disdain. So giving was his heart, not even the boundaries of space and time kept him from reaching out to others in need. Day in and day out,

Martin gave his all for others out of a love for them rooted in his love of God. For Martin knew that, like Jesus, we are called to respond to people in need not because they "deserve" our help by some merit of their own, but because it is what God calls us to do, because the person before us is a child of God, the face of Christ before us, even if nothing this person does or has done seems "deserving."

responding together

Other times what holds us back from giving is that the problems are so big they overwhelm and paralyze us into inaction. We know that even if we help this one homeless person, two more will need help tomorrow. If we serve at a food kitchen, we will see the same faces the next day and the next and the next. If we recycle, bike to work and minimize our energy use, environmental problems will still loom as large and per- plexing tomorrow as they do today. When what we do seems inconse- quential in the grand scheme of things, it is tempting to give up, forget about the problems and let someone else deal with them.

In Martin's time there were such seemingly unsolvable problems, too. In the face of the fate of the lost children of Lima, the citizens had thrown in the towel, deemed it a lost cause and turned a blind eye. What could be done? There were so many children and with such need— clothing, food, housing, education, health care—the situation appeared hopeless.

But Martin was a person of hope and faith, and he knew this prob- lem was too important to ignore. He knew what it was like to be an unwanted child and he couldn't ignore those children's needs. He began by praying over the situation. Many might consider this start a waste of time, but it was through prayer that he came upon a solution. It wasn't a solution he could accomplish on his own; it was a solution that required communal action. Starting with raising awareness, he made the citizens see the problem they had been ignoring, and acknowledge that it was unacceptable to abandon these children. When people's consciences were prodded and they were moved to respond in action, he offered a vision of what could help improve the situation and how everyone could contribute. With a vision and a solution, people responded generously and a fully staffed orphanage and school was built.

The problems in the world are too big for one person to tackle. But we are not here alone, we are here together, and when faced together, problems are still challenging but much more manageable. Sometimes we may be called to be the Martins of the world and raise people's awareness and prompt them to action. Sometimes we will hear the message from the Martins of this world on the news, through our friends or at work, and we will have the choice to ignore, criticize or respond and become engaged. The choice is never easy and there is plenty of disagreement to go around. But what remains critical is to keep praying for the inspiration to face the problems of today and not to give up the hope that together we can make a difference.

REFLECTION QUESTIONS

How do you think about the poor and homeless? What are the thoughts that come to you when you meet them? How do you respond to their call for help?

How do you treat the poor when you help them? With understanding? Joy? Compassion? Or with superiority? Cynicism? Pity? How do you respond when you know you've been taken advantage of?

What are some of the problems that overwhelm you into inaction? Have you ever brought them to prayer and talked to God about them? How has God responded?

Have you ever had Martin's leading role in addressing a social problem in your community? How was your experience similar and how was it different? What did you learn from it?

Is there someone in your life now trying to get you to see a particular problem and move you to action? What is this person's message and how are you responding so far? Do you think God is urging you to think about this problem through this person? How so?

ELIZABETH ANN SETON

embracing our suffering

Father, into your hands I commend my spirit.

—Luke 23:46b

Elizabeth Ann Seton's life can read like a litany of suffering, loss and hardship. A lonely child whose mother died while she was still a toddler, she would face bankruptcy, the death of her husband, rejection when she embraced the Catholic faith and the heartbreaking death of two of her own children and three of her sisters-in-law who were near and dear to her. But all this tragedy neither embittered nor paralyzed her into despair. This ever-gracious woman continued to thoughtfully respond to God's call in her life, reaching an ever-deeper level of trust in God through each challenge life threw her way, offering us an example of how we too can grow and move forward through the adversities and sufferings we experience in our own lives.

childhood and youth

On August 28, 1774, Richard Bayley and Catherine Charlton welcomed their second daughter, Elizabeth, into the world in New York. While

Elizabeth was still a toddler, her mother died, followed a few years later by Elizabeth's baby sister. Despite her young age, Elizabeth later recalled, "sitting alone on a step of the doorway looking at the clouds, while my little sister Catherine, two years old, lay in her coffin; they asked me: did I not cry when little Kitty was dead? No, because Kitty is gone up to heaven. I wish I could go too with mamma."[11]

The loneliness expressed in her words pervaded most of Elizabeth's childhood. Her father remarried, but Elizabeth never found in her new family the love and sense of belonging for which she longed. Finding her efforts at friendship continually rejected by her stepfamily, Elizabeth spent many hours alone and became introspective. In her loneliness she discovered an interior harbor of peace where she found comfort in the experience of God as the One Changeless Being in a changing and uncertain world. As she matured into a teenager, Elizabeth continued spending time alone, meditating, reflecting on God, taking walks by herself and devoting time for spiritual reading and prayer, even though her calendar was filled with all the typical activities of the time.

It was also during these teenage years that Elizabeth fell in love. William Magee Seton, Jr., was a charming, well-grounded and honest man from a prosperous shipping family. They met when Elizabeth was sixteen and William twenty-two, and they married four years later. Newly married and pregnant and with a home of her own, Elizabeth could not imagine greater joy: "My own home at twenty.—The world and heaven too, quite impossible!"[12] The young couple's bliss only grew with the birth of Anna Maria on May 3, 1795, and William the following year. Three more children would come: Richard, Catherine and Rebecca.

challenges of family life

The stretch of peaceful happiness was short-lived. The first scare came when young William became so ill that it was doubtful he would survive. Until his recovery Elizabeth was terrified she would lose him and was anguished that she should have known the joy of motherhood only to watch her child suffer such an ill fate. But William recovered and this time the threat of loss momentarily passed.

The shadow of loss would not spare Elizabeth for long. Her husband's father slipped on ice during the winter of 1798; he never recovered and died that June, leaving William and Elizabeth responsible for William's seven siblings still living at home. Overburdened with household and work duties (Elizabeth was helping William with his business), Elizabeth worked tirelessly to tend to everyone's needs.

But the family's troubles were only just beginning. William, Sr., had been a gifted businessman and unfortunately none of the remaining partners in the company were quite as skilled. Combined with the loss of a number of ships to pirates, this soon translated into total financial loss. As the months progressed, the scope of the economic loss continued to emerge. Despite the worries of a mother on a budget with young children, Elizabeth did not fall into despair or become paralyzed with depression. The situation finally hit bottom when William declared bankruptcy and the family moved to a more affordable neighborhood.

As a consequence of the shipping firm's financial decline, one of William's associates (also a distant relative) was sent to jail, leaving his family bereft. Never ones to deny assistance to others regardless of the suffering and difficulty to which they might themselves be prey, Elizabeth and William opened their home to the family. This generosity added to Elizabeth's already heavy burden, but she never complained. Her charitable work made her only too aware that others suffered more than she did.

spiritual growth

As the family adjusted to its new situation, Elizabeth's spiritual life took a significant step forward. So far Elizabeth had grown in her spiritual journey without much guidance. She had made great strides in her relationship with God but had constructed a rather eclectic system of beliefs in the process, one that drew from various traditions: She wore a crucifix, believed in angels, liked Methodist hymns and practiced Quaker quietism while attending Episcopalian services. When a new pastor by the name of John Henry Hobart arrived at the Episcopalian Trinity Church where Elizabeth attended services, his passionate zeal for the gospel appealed to her. While he became her first spiritual role model and mentor, she became one of his staunch supporters, especially where charitable works were concerned.

Guided by Hobart, Elizabeth reached a significant spiritual moment in her journey toward surrender to God: "*Sunday, 12th August* [1802].—Three weeks and two days after the birth of my Rebecca I renewed my covenant that I would strive with myself and use every earnest endeavor to serve my dear Redeemer and to give myself wholly unto Him."[13] When she received the sacrament of the Eucharist soon after, she interpreted it as "the seal of the covenant which I trust will not be broken in life or in death, in time or in eternity."[14] This understanding blossomed into a profound devotion to the Episcopalian remembrance of the Last Supper.

a spouse's loss

From the time they met, William had shown symptoms of tuberculosis, a disease that ran in his family. Now in its final stage, there was little that could be done. Hoping to buy more time, William and Elizabeth traveled to Leghorn, Italy, to visit the Filicchi family, business friends of William's. Anna, who was eight at the time, traveled with them while arrangements were made for the children who stayed behind.

The voyage had a positive effect on William's health and provided Elizabeth with needed rest and time to read and reflect. But when they arrived in Italy on November 18, 1803, they found themselves in possibly the worst imaginable situation. Although the latest bout of yellow fever had died down in New York before their departure, their ship brought news of the outbreak, and the Setons were quarantined for a month in a small, cold room with grated windows and little furniture other than a mattress on the floor. The Filicchis provided them with a bed and benches and sent food; they, the ship's captain and Elizabeth's brother Carleton, who was in Italy at the time, all visited regularly. But needless to say, William's health spiraled downward.

Elizabeth struggled to console herself and her daughter that God was with them and everything would turn out all right. In her Leghorn journal, along with the private tears and pain, her husband's physical decline, her and Anna's fear, she also shared her faith in divine providence, the new-found closeness with William found through shared prayer and spiritual reading and the joy of the interior transformation she witnessed in her husband. When the confinement ended on December 19, it was too late for William; he died at peace the morning of December 27, leaving the twenty-nine-year-old Elizabeth to raise their five children alone and with no financial resources.

In her Leghorn journal Elizabeth shared the following words about William: "No one ever knew my William without giving him the quality of an amiable man; but to see him exalted to the peaceful, humble Christian waiting the will of God with patience that seems more than human, and a firm faith that would do honor to the most distinguished piety, is a happiness allowed only to the wife and mother, who is separated from all other happiness connected with this scene of things."[15]

embracing catholicism

In this time of mourning and loss, the Filicchi family warmly welcomed and cared for Elizabeth and Anna. The two brothers—Filippo and Antonio—and their families were taken with the young widow whose exceptional character and inner beauty were apparent to all. They extended such sincere friendship that Anna could exclaim, "Oh, mamma! how many friends God has provided for us in this strange land, for they are our friends before they know us."[16]

Years later Elizabeth also suffered the deaths of three of the sisters-in-law that had been under her care since the death of William's father: Rebecca, Cecilia and Harriett.

The Filicchis were also Elizabeth's first real contact with Catholics. Kind and generous, Elizabeth admired their devotion to prayer and fasting and the sincerity of their faith. When she displayed an openness to dialogue and an interest in the pursuit of truth, they began to share their faith with her, encouraging and guiding her in her exploration. Elizabeth's search revealed a wealth of spiritual beliefs and practices— Catholic devotion to the Blessed Mother, the celebration of Lent as a season of real fasting and penance, the simple blessing with the Sign of the Cross, which touched her searching heart. But nothing moved Elizabeth more profoundly than her growing appreciation for the Eucharist:

> ...how happy we would be if we believed what these good souls believe, that they *possess God* in the Sacrament, and that He remains in their churches, and is carried to them when they are sick. Ah! me. When they carry the Blessed Sacrament under my window, while I feel the full loneliness and sadness of my case, I can not stop the tears at the thought. My God! how happy would I be, even so far away from all so dear, if I could find you in the church, as they do! (for there is a chapel in the very house of Mr. Filicchi); how many things I would say to you of the sorrows of my heart and the sins of my life.[17]

Before Elizabeth was ready to take the final plunge into the Catholic church, the time had come for her to return to New York. Unwilling to see Elizabeth and Anna travel alone, Antonio took the opportunity to travel to the United States for business, hoping also to see the work of Elizabeth's conversion brought to completion. When they arrived in New York on June 4, 1804, Elizabeth had to depend on the hospitality of others for food and shelter for herself and her children. Not wishing to accept such kindness under false pretenses and aware of the bias against Catholics among New York's social elite at the time, Elizabeth did not hide the fact that she was seriously considering embracing this faith.

Initially, none of her friends and family turned their backs on her, some of them believing it was a product of her sorrow and she would soon abandon this disgraceful pursuit. Yet Elizabeth persevered in her inquiry.

Concerned for her spiritual state, Hobart and others endeavored to persuade her to remain in the Episcopal church, and the reading material and discussion they shared gave her pause. Paralyzed by indecision, Elizabeth remained ambivalent for months until she broke through the standstill the following January. Despairing over her inner turmoil, she sought solace in an Episcopalian service. As she herself shared with Antonio's wife, Amelia, "if I left the house a Protestant, I returned to it a Catholic I think,"[18] for the ritual only heightened for her the shortcomings she perceived in the Episcopal faith: the lack of apostolic succession and its implications for the sacramental forgiveness of sins, but most importantly, the lack of belief in the Real Presence. A few months later Elizabeth made her profession of faith in the Catholic church and her first confession a week later before receiving her First Communion on March 25, a profound and unforgettable experience.

Hostility in New York came to a head when the sixteen-year-old Cecilia Seton announced her intention of following in Elizabeth's footsteps and becoming Catholic. The Seton family was horrified by the prospect that one of their own would sink to such a distasteful level (Elizabeth was, after all, just an in-law) and pressured her mercilessly to recant. On the day her family was going to disown her, Cecilia left on her own accord, turning to Elizabeth for refuge before fulfilling her desire. The news of Elizabeth's influence on Cecilia's conversion spread all over town, causing a terrible uproar and backlash.

adjusting to a new home

The change in religious affiliation affected every aspect of Elizabeth's life. Socially speaking, although her dear friends and her sister accepted her decision and continued to assist her, she experienced a decided change in attitude from many past acquaintances, friends and even her in-laws. In terms of work, her attempts to support her family were increasingly hampered given her religious background and she intermittently had to rely on the financial generosity of Antonio, her friend Julia Scott and her sister to make ends meet.

But as doors of her past life closed, new ones began to open. In November 1806 a new priest arrived at Elizabeth's parish. When they finally sat down to chat over coffee, Elizabeth poured out her secret desire to join a convent and possibly teach after the boys had finished school. Much to her surprise, Father William Dubourg asked, "Why wait?" With his help and that of two Boston-area priests of his acquaintance, Elizabeth and her children left New York on June 9, 1808, bound for Baltimore. There Dubourg had arranged a teaching position for her and a good educational opportunity for her boys. Despite the hostility she had experienced in New York because of her faith, the city had been Elizabeth's home for many years and she was sad to leave.

The family immediately felt welcomed to their new city, a heartwarming change from New York. After settling into their new home next to St. Mary's Church, Elizabeth began teaching in the fall. The idea was to begin a school and to found a religious community as soon as such a venture was feasible. Even before the necessary funds for the foundation were obtained in 1808, there were already young women interested in joining Elizabeth.

A location in Emmitsburg, Maryland, was selected for the community and preparations of the site and plans for the foundation slowly started taking shape. On March 25, 1809, the Feast of the Annunciation, Elizabeth took vows of poverty, chastity and obedience before Archbishop John Carroll and set out for Emmitsburg in June with the small number of women who joined her.

This was the birth of the first community of women religious native to the United States. They would take the name Sisters of St. Joseph (known later as the Daughters of Charity of St. Joseph), and

Elizabeth would be the first mother superior and first headmistress of the school they opened in the fall. The school would become a parochial school and the educational enterprise would develop into the Catholic parochial school system.

By the time of Elizabeth's death, the community of the Daughters of Charity of St. Joseph numbered more than fifty sisters and had already expanded to Philadelphia and New York. It would continue to grow in the coming years, opening orphanages, hospitals and schools.

> Elizabeth encouraged her sisters in community not to be satisfied with spiritual mediocrity: "Why are we not saints?... Because we do not watch over our interior, do not watch over the impulse of nature and grace in our actions, nor avoid the occasions of the habitual faults in which we live when it is in our power, or keep a good guard on ourselves when it is not."[19]

a mother's loss

The sisters endured many hardships and trials during those early years, but none was harder on Elizabeth than the loss of her beloved Anna. In the winter of 1811 and 1812 Anna fell ill and Elizabeth suspected tuberculosis. They had grown very close and openly discussed their impending separation with courage and peaceful acceptance. After fulfilling her desire to be received into the community—the first sister to do so under the new rules and constitutions—Anna died on March 12 at the age of sixteen.

Although Elizabeth had faced Anna's illness with resolve, the reality of her death and absence was almost unbearable. In a letter to a friend Elizabeth shared the difficulty of the months that followed: "For three months after Nina [Anna] was taken I was so often expecting to lose my senses, and my head was so disordered,

> With her sisters in community, Elizabeth shared her commitment to the will of God: "And what was the first rule of our dear Saviour's life? You know it was to do His Father's will. Well, then, the first end I propose in our daily work is to do the will of God; secondly, to do it in the manner He wills; and thirdly, to do it because it is His will."[20]

that unless for the daily duties always before me, I did not know much what I did or what I left undone."[21] Yet even in this desolation, Elizabeth continued to trust in God, expressing her confidence in the words of Jesus: "Father, into Thy Hands I commend My Spirit."[22]

The peace of heart and absolute confidence in God with which Elizabeth embraced Rebecca's death only a few years later reveals that Elizabeth's journey of surrender to the divine will was complete. The year after Anna's death, Rebecca took a bad fall on some ice. She was ten years old at the time and, not wishing to cause worry or concern, hid the seriousness of her injury. By the time Elizabeth recognized the severity of her condition, the injury was irreversible. Rebecca's health continued to decline until all she could do was sit on her mother's lap, whose arm and leg grew almost atrophied from holding her. Elizabeth held her daughter through the time of her death on November 3, 1816, at the age of fourteen.

Elizabeth knew that her own death would come earlier rather than later. Her health had not been perfect for many years, and five years prior she had finally admitted to herself she too had tuberculosis and would one day share the fate of so many of her loved ones. Despite the shadow on the horizon, Elizabeth devoted herself wholeheartedly to her role as headmistress, mother superior and mother to her three surviving children until her death on January 4, 1821, at the age of forty-six.

Elizabeth Seton was beatified in 1963 by Pope John XXIII and canonized in 1975 by Pope Paul VI. She is the patron saint of widows, orphans and parents who have lost a child. A shrine in her honor was built in Emmitsburg, Maryland, where her remains are buried.

REFLECTION
experiencing suffering

A lonely childhood, family rejection, loss of fortune, social standing and prestige, death of parents, spouse, two children and three close sisters-in-law, falling prey to an illness that afflicted many loved ones—for most of us, dealing with one or two of these tragedies would pose a significant challenge. When we are the ones who get the pink slip and spend months unsuccessfully looking for a job as the bills keep coming, when we are the ones at the doctor's office listening to the ominous diagnosis, when we are the ones at the front of the receiving line in the funeral home, when we are the ones who have become a pariah in our social or work community, the words *suffering* and *loss* take on a whole new level of meaning.

Even if the loss was foreseeable and we had time to prepare for it, nothing can really prepare us for the emotional impact of the lived reality of our loss. Intellectually we may know and have read all about the grieving process, the ups and downs of the job search, the various possible outcomes of the feared disease. But it is one thing to know intellectually what is coming—the sadness, discouragement, stress—and another to experience what it's like to be truly unable to get out of bed in the morning, to burst into tears in public places, to be afraid to open the mail or pick up the phone lest it be one more thing that will remind us of our situation. The emptiness, the dejection, the isolation can easily and quickly take over, consuming and blinding us to all but the unbearable pain of our loss.

facing our suffering

Elizabeth had a foot poised in this abyss on more than one occasion. The possibility of her son William's death as an infant made her question why God would bless someone with such a gift only to take it away; the loss of her beloved Anna so overwhelmed her that she feared she might lose her sanity. But even though her various trials challenged her faith, Elizabeth still came to the end of her life with trust and confidence in the goodness of God.

To many of us, surrendering to God might sound like resignation and giving up, a response everything in and around us tells us we should not embrace. On the contrary, we believe we should do all in our power to overcome and prevail against the trials life throws our way. We look at hardship as life's or God's way of trying to push us down, of keeping us from being too happy—as if there were a limit to how much happiness there is to go around and how much each of us is entitled to have—and look at our response as our way of showing life, showing God, that we are not so easily defeated.

But surrendering to God is not about resignation or giving up. As Elizabeth embraced each trial and loss, she did not sit back waiting for the next calamity to hit her; she rallied her energy to discern the next step forward and continued on as best she could for as long as she could. Surrender to God is about recognizing that our view of life is limited, greatly so, in comparison to what God's view must be like. Surrender to God is about recognizing we cannot really escape our humanity—ourselves, our times, our places—whereas God can see and understand all, making our perspectives a lot different. Elizabeth understood that a Christian's surrender to God is about following in Jesus' footsteps of embracing the cross. In the face of suffering, hardship and defeat, when all seems lost and God seems absent, surrender to God is about continuing to trust and believe that, despite all evidence to the contrary, God is still with us and that when we embrace our suffering, we fall into the embrace of a God who raises us up to new life—a life in which the scars of our pain are not erased or denied, but transformed into a sign of hope.

embracing our suffering

When hardship strikes, determined not to be defeated, we rally our forces, and we turn to our network of support and to experts when necessary. Sometimes our efforts pay off and we emerge victorious—we get an even better job, we meet someone else, we beat cancer. But we will not always be victorious; the day comes when our efforts are like beating our head against the wall. That is the day we come face to face with what we *really* believe about life, about ourselves, about what it means to be human, about God. That is the day we cannot escape our anger or serenity, our resentment and sense of injustice before what we stand to lose or the duration of the gratitude we feel, our clenched hearts determined to hold on or the open heart that is willing to journey into the unknown. That is the day we realize whether or not we do believe that the cross ends in failure as it seemed in the eyes of the world, or in the victory of the resurrection as it did in the eyes of the faithful.

For the cross that is at the heart of our faith is a cross that leads to resurrection, but a resurrection brought about by God's action, not ours. Whatever the outcome of our struggles, at the heart of our faith lies the challenging but inspiring claim that although God has not chosen to spare us the suffering that comes our way, God *has* chosen to walk through our suffering with us and to piece us back together and breathe new life into us. It took Elizabeth many years and much hardship to come to a place where she could fully surrender to God and embrace the fullness of the mystery of the cross in the footsteps of Jesus. It is not an easy path, not a path any of us want to travel. But when suffering inevitably comes our way, traveling through it in the footsteps of Jesus as Elizabeth did is daring to trust that God will also share with us the promise of fullness of life that lies beyond.

REFLECTION QUESTIONS

What have been some of the greatest hardships you have faced? How did you make your way through them? What are some of the things you learned about yourself, about life, about God through your suffering?

How do you respond to hardship, suffering or loss? Who and what helps you through?

How have you experienced God in the midst of hardship, suffering and loss?

What have been some of your experiences of resurrection? How did they come about? What did you learn about yourself, about life, about God through your experiences of resurrection?

nine

KATHARINE DREXEL

becoming what we celebrate

Then he took a cup, and after giving thanks he said, "Take this and divide it among yourselves...." Then he took a loaf of bread, and when he had given thanks, he broke it and gave it to them, saying, "This is my body, which is given for you. Do this in remembrance of me."

—Luke 22:17, 19

Born to a wealthy, loving family with a strong devotion to the Eucharist and service to those in greatest need, Katharine Drexel shared her family legacy with those neglected by society. After years of discernment, this American saint formed a religious community centered on devotion to the Eucharist. This devotion had nurtured her from childhood to go forth and be the presence of Christ to the Native American and African American communities—the abandoned and forgotten of society. This much-needed work was a labor of joyful love, one Katharine embarked upon undaunted by the challenges and dangers of the racially divided times, which brought to life the true meaning of the Eucharist to which she was so devoted.

family life

Katharine was born on November 26, 1858, in Philadelphia, Pennsylvania, to Frank Drexel and Hannah Jane Langstroth. Hannah passed away soon after Katharine's birth and two years later, Frank Drexel married Emma Bouvier, the woman Katharine would know as her mother. Three years later a little sister, Louise, was born, joining Katharine and her older sister, Elizabeth, completing the close-knit family that lovingly nurtured its members on their respective paths to sanctity.

Following the example her mother had given in her own home, Emma set aside a room in their Philadelphia home to be used for prayer. It was in this sacred space that the family gathered nightly before retiring to bed, and where each found a private and quiet place to pray during the day. Both Emma and Frank had a deep devotion to the Blessed Sacrament, and through their example passed this devotion on to their children.

Although the Drexel family was enormously wealthy, Frank and Emma did not allow their family to become subservient to material possessions. Rather, they used their financial wealth to help those less fortunate than themselves and inculcated in their children a deep sense of responsibility for the welfare of others that comes with such wealth and position. Emma taught the girls about charity and service by bringing them on her visits to poor neighborhoods and engaging them in the work of direct assistance to the needy, sometimes expecting them to help out of their own pockets. Frank Drexel supported and encouraged Emma's charitable work and he himself took a

Emma also saw to it that the girls contributed to the running of their summer house, assigning them responsibilities proportionate to their ages and abilities: Elizabeth supervised the kitchen and stables, Katharine the general housework, and Louise the barn and grounds.

behind-the-scenes approach to charity by sitting on numerous boards and contributing generously to the financial needs of the organizations in which he was involved.

discernment years

When she was twenty, Katharine completed her formal education and made her debut in society. She was a well-liked young woman and had a busy social life. But the whirlwind of fun was short-lived. Later that year Emma was diagnosed with cancer. During the three years of illness that ended with Emma's death, Katharine and her sister Elizabeth shared the nursing duties. While caring for their mother, the young women pondered their futures and struggled to discern their vocations. Elizabeth came to believe her vocation was to serve God in the world, as a layperson, for it was here she believed she could do the most good; Katharine, who had previously been certain she did not have a vocation to the religious life, suddenly found herself contemplating the possibility that she did in fact have such a vocation.

Uncertain about this important decision, Katharine turned to her spiritual director for guidance. Bishop James O'Connor of Nebraska had been Katharine's spiritual director since he'd been assigned as pastor to a parish in the vicinity of the Drexel summer home when Katharine was about thirteen. In response to Katharine's plea, he suggested she employ the Ignatian method of discernment. After receiving Katharine's list of the pros and cons, O'Connor counseled further reflection based on the abstract and impersonal reasons she gave in favor of entering religious life. After continued correspondence, he expressed the belief she might have a vocation to celibacy and proposed she test this possibility by making a yearlong vow of virginity, a suggestion Katharine quietly and secretly followed.

In September 1884, another dimension of what would become Katharine's vocation began to blossom. As a result of a family trip out west, Katharine took the first step of translating her interest in the plight of the Native Americans into action. During the trip the family stopped at a mission church in Tacoma, Washington, that served the Native American population in the area. It was a small church and the community could not afford a statue of the Blessed Mother. Upon her return home, Katharine purchased one for them using half her considerable monthly allowance. This extravagant generosity was only the beginning of what would become Katharine's life's work.

Another painful loss soon visited the Drexel sisters when Frank Drexel died suddenly of a massive heart attack the following year. Deeply affected by this new loss, Katharine's health deteriorated and her worried sisters took her to Europe, hoping the change of scenery would help restore her strength. During the trip something unexpected happened. After an audience with Pope Leo XIII, Katharine asked for and was granted a private word with him. Her purpose was to pass on a request from Bishop O'Connor for more missionary priests to the Native American population in the western territories. The pope's response to her impassioned petition was to ask, "Why not, my child, yourself become a missionary?"[23] The question surprised Katharine and added further confusion to her attempt to discern her vocation.

Their beloved father gone, the three sisters were suddenly left the heiresses of an enormous estate, one they proceeded to use as their parents had taught them: in assistance to those in need. Elizabeth worked on providing vocational training to orphaned boys, establishing a school to do so; Katharine continued to increase her involvement in and support of Native American missions; Louise became devoted to service to the African American community. Through all their ventures, the sisters remained close mutual allies.

Bishop O'Connor continued to affirm his conviction that Katharine's vocation was to serve God in the world as she was currently doing. But after years of discernment, Katharine finally wrote to him humbly expressing her own certainty that she had a vocation to the religious life and begging for his blessing in pursuing this path. Swayed by her persistence, Bishop O'Connor finally gave his blessing and at the age of thirty, Katharine set about deciding what order to enter. She shared the strong devotion to the Blessed Sacrament her parents had demonstrated and wished to enter an order that allowed frequent reception of the Eucharist. She also had a strong commitment to the apostolate to the Native Americans, but was inclined toward a contemplative rather than an active order. None of the suggestions Bishop O'Connor proposed offered this particular combination.

Hitting on what was certainly a divinely inspired plan, Bishop O'Connor came personally to propose a new possibility to Katharine: Why not start a new religious order whose mission was to serve the two most needy communities—Native Americans and African Americans? Katharine was less than thrilled by the suggestion. She did not believe she had the necessary qualities to be the founder of a religious order, nor was she convinced the foundation of a new order was the best way to serve these communities. But Bishop O'Connor was utterly convinced as his words to Katharine reflect: "I was never so sure of any vocation, not even my own, as I am of yours. If you do not establish the order in question, you will allow to pass an opportunity of doing immense service to the Church which may not occur again."[24] Finally persuaded by Bishop O'Connor's plan, Katharine began her formation with the Mercy Sisters of Pittsburgh.

In the time that Katharine had been discerning her vocation, her sisters had been pursuing their own. Louise married Edward Morrell, a man who shared her concern for the rights and needs of African Americans, and together they assisted Katharine on this apostolate. Elizabeth also married but died near the end of her first pregnancy. Walter Smith, her widower, served pro bono as counsel to Katharine's congregation for thirty-three years.

foundation of a new order

Having sparked the plan for a new religious order, Bishop O'Connor unfortunately did not live to see Katharine bring it to fruition. On May 27, 1890, the man who had guided her for so many years passed away after a few months of declining health. Katharine was crushed: It had been Bishop O'Connor who had encouraged her through her continued doubts, and now she found herself alone with them. But in this dark hour God provided a new shoulder for her to lean on, one who would guide her through the years of foundation. After presiding at Bishop O'Connor's funeral in Omaha, Archbishop John Ryan of Philadelphia stopped to visit Katharine. In response to her heartfelt doubts, he responded, "If I share the burden with you, if I help you, can you go on?"[25] It was just the encouragement Katharine needed.

During its early years, the community received threats of violence and experienced numerous incidents born out of the strong racial prejudice, hatred and tension prevalent at the time. But the sisters persevered in their mission to the African American community, sometimes resorting to subterfuge and sometimes seeming to be spared or aided by providence.

Katharine made her final profession on February 12, 1891, simultaneously establishing the new order and becoming known as Mother Katharine, foundress. The date had been carefully chosen for its significance: It was both the anniversary of the profession of Mother Catherine McAuley, founder of the Sisters of Charity, who had provided Katharine her formation, and the birth date of Abraham Lincoln. The name of the order, the Sisters of the Blessed Sacrament for Indians and Colored People, had been chosen just as carefully to reflect its spirituality and mission: Rooted in their devotion to the Blessed Sacrament, the sisters would then go out to bring Christ to the two most needy communities.

One of the first questions confronted by the new congregation was whether or not to accept African American postulants. Although it might seem that given their mission they should of course do so, they initially decided against it. The few existing African American orders in the South were struggling to attract new postulants and the new order did not want to compete for candidates. In addition, an integrated community in the cultural milieu of the late nineteenth century seemed untenable. When the congregation began accepting African American candidates in the 1950s, it was still a step ahead of the times.

Another issue that surfaced early on was the financial stability of the order and its work. Through the early years Katharine provided most of the financial support needed for the establishment of convents and schools. But as was stipulated in her father's will, Katharine did not have access to the estate's principal, only to the funds distributed to date. This meant that upon Katharine's death, the order would lose its main source of funding and would be left to face an uncertain future given that its mission was not the most popular or best supported. Anxious to face the future prepared, Bishop O'Connor had recommended that Katharine set up an endowment for the order by setting aside a portion of her yearly income. Katharine initially refused. She took the vow of poverty very seriously and believed the community should share the poverty of those they served, trusting God would provide for their needs. But eventually, the governing council prevailed upon Katharine to take some steps to help ensure the future of the order she had established through life insurance policies. Given the imminent possibility of death, either through violence or a deadly disease caught while making a trip to the western missions, such planning was a prudent option.

In the course of its first five years, the community opened its first two schools, establishing its ministry on solid ground. St. Catherine's, a school serving Native Americans in the Santa Fe region, opened in the fall of 1894; "Rock Castle," serving the needs of African American girls, opened in Virginia in 1899. The community envisioned education of Native Americans and African Americans as its primary

Katharine always had a strong devotion to the Eucharist and shared some of her reflections on the sacrament: "In Holy Communion the life of God in a particular way is imparted to my soul. It is there that God becomes the soul of my soul, to do, to suffer, all for love of Him who died for me, and if Thou art for me, if Thou art within me, what can I fear, O my God?"[26]

means of serving these populations by helping to develop leaders among them who could take an active role in society. Furthermore, they approached education not simply as instruction but as a venture to foster the overall flourishing and growth of the students. This wholesome approach led them to visit the students' families, especially the sick and the imprisoned, recognizing that meeting these greater needs was just as important to fostering the students' development as teaching was. This approach was one of the hallmarks of the sisters' ministry and offered an example of Christian living that spoke more loudly to the students than any indoctrination could.

Mother Mercedes, Katharine's successor as superior general of the order, recalled, "And with all this, Mother was as full of merriment, happiness and joy; she was as young as the youngest postulant among us at recreation and her keen sense of humor saw the ridiculous and humorous in many situations."[27]

In 1915 Katharine began what was probably her crowning achievement: the establishment of Xavier University in Louisiana, the first ever Catholic African American university. Adding to Xavier's uniqueness was its coeducational, integrated faculty. The enterprise proved a resounding success and the labor and investment in it bore much fruit by forming a new crop of teachers to serve in the growing number of schools the community opened.

from action to contemplation

Over the coming years Katharine maintained a nonstop schedule. Always available to help with the manual labor required in preparation for the opening of a school, to welcome and meet new candidates, and for personal meetings with her sisters, Katherine alternately traveled west to visit and inspect mission schools and south and east to build new ones. Yet this burdensome labor never seemed to diminish her joy and delight in life, her humility and deep reverence and respect for her fellow children of God—whatever their race. And it was these personal qualities that touched and transformed those who met her.

Eventually, the hectic pace caught up with her aging body and in 1934 Katharine suffered her first heart attack at the age of seventy-six. She cut back on her work to a degree, but that was not enough. She suffered another attack the following year. As her health continued to decline, she stepped down from her role as superior general, taking on the duties of vicar general until she was too weak to fulfill these as well. Eventually she only had strength for prayer and contemplation, finally becoming the contemplative she had initially longed to be. Surviving so many loved ones was Katharine's only sorrow, but one for which she always found consolation in the Eucharist, a celebration through which she came together with all those who now watched over her.

> A teacher hired to train the sisters commented of Katharine, "The day I went there and she hired me, I said, 'She's a saint if I ever saw one.' And I never changed my opinion."[28]

Having given her fortune, her time, her life for those in greatest need, Katharine died on March 2, 1955, at the age of ninety-two, leaving behind sixty-three schools and five hundred sisters. Many of the young novices did not really know who Katharine was and were surprised by the outpouring of mourners at the news of her death—men, women and children of all walks of life who had been touched by the loving example of this wonderful woman who had embodied the meaning of self-gift she had been nurtured with at the Eucharist for so many years.

> Katharine Drexel was declared blessed on November 20, 1988, and added to the canon of saints on October 1, 2000, by Pope John Paul II. Her remains lie at her shrine in St. Elizabeth's convent in Bensalem, Pennsylvania, outside of Philadelphia.

REFLECTION
why go to mass?

As the weekend arrives and our plans unfold, the question of Mass *should* come up. To go or not to go; when to go; do I *have* to go? There are so many tempting reasons not to go and we all know plenty of people who seem only too happy to remind us of them on a frequent basis. And they have a point. Most of us have been to our share of Masses at which the music was off-key, the lector sounded like she was reading the Scriptures for the first time or as if reading the morning paper. Then there's the priest who bears the brunt of the criticism: The homily was too harsh or too liberal, too intellectual or too touchy-feely, he didn't talk to the kids, he ignored the teens, or he talked to the adults as if they were kids. And let's not forget ourselves, the mumbling assembly moving through the ritual more worried about when it will be over so we can take off and go about the rest of our busy days than we are about what it is we're doing and saying. We try; we do. But let's face it, the overall consensus out there seems to be that Mass is just flat-out boring.

So when the weekend rolls around, staying in and enjoying the morning peace and quiet sounds like heaven; a walk in the park if it's a nice day to feel at one with nature and God sounds much more appealing; a run along the trail seems just what we need to lift our spirits. Yes, the "I can pray to God by myself just as well" club has its draw. So does the megachurch down the street. With its spectacular sound system, large screens, welcoming committee, social coffee hour and crowded parking lot, they seem much more fun and with it. Yes, the grass does look greener everywhere else.

becoming a eucharistic people

At a time when Mass was celebrated in Latin, probably no less "boring" than it is today, Katharine wanted to go to Mass every day, wanting to receive Communion. Frequent reception of Communion was in fact so important and meaningful to Katharine that she hesitated joining a religious community that did not embrace this practice, even though it was an unusual one at the time.

This devotion to the Eucharist was nurtured in Katharine from a young age by the witness and example of her parents. It was not an empty devotion performed out of duty, obligation or even for the sake of appearances. The depth of their devotion to the Eucharist found its fulfillment in the eucharistic lives they lived, the way they became in the world the Christ they adored and received at Mass. It was this critical connection between the Eucharist and daily life that formed Katharine's devotion and life. Centered in the prayer of the church, the Drexels went out in service to the world, service to those in greatest need, performed with humility, compassion, generosity, reverence and respect, service born out of the recognition that the gifts given are meant to be shared for the common good.

Throughout her own life, Katharine also embraced this connection. Always rooted in the celebration, sharing and adoration of the Eucharist, Katherine spent many years pondering how God was calling her to share and become the Christ she devoutly received. A debutante with a busy social calendar who could have led a carefree life of unending engagements and pastimes, Katharine not only sought to meet the needs of the disenfranchised and abandoned by society, she ultimately hungered to be the sacrament of Christ for them. Katharine was an instrument of transformation in the lives of countless people not just because of her long list of accomplishments in the work of social justice, but also because of her very presence, one that undeniably reflected the presence of Christ.

how could we not go to mass?

The celebration of the Eucharist is not meant to be an hour of entertainment. God is not there to put on a flashy show that will raise the roof, and we're not there to watch one. The celebration of the Eucharist is an action, one that requires our participation, one that begins and ends out there, beyond the parking lot. In the weekly celebration of the Eucharist, we are called to bring forth the work of our human hands— the work we've been so busy doing all week—to be offered in praise and thanksgiving to the God through whose goodness we even have this gift we often complain about, but for which we are ultimately grateful. We are invited to take and receive what we came with, a gift now blessed, broken, shared and transformed by the Risen, living Christ into his own body to be broken and shared with those who most need to experience the real presence of Christ.

This action that is the Eucharist is not one performed by a multitude of individuals who just happen to be in the same room at the same time doing the same thing. Rather, the Eucharist is celebrated by a communion made one by a bond that transcends time and space. The celebration of the Eucharist requires that all those gathered move, speak, sing, listen and pray as one body in this sacred place that we may always be strengthened, as Katharine was, by the bond we share with those who stand with us.

This kind of active participation that embraces the celebration of the Eucharist as an action that encompasses the entirety of our lives doesn't happen by accident; it demands conscious intentionality and purpose, the sincere desire to become the fullness of what we celebrate. If we could all truly live in such a manner, we could never think of the Mass as boring. It doesn't take flashy gimmicks or even flawless perfection for the Mass to raise the roof—that would actually be easy. It takes each one of us, all of us, living our lives as the Eucharist, sharing the Christ we receive with those who are hungry for him. Then, if asked, "Why do you go to Mass?" we wouldn't fumble for a response, we would simply say, "How can I not go? It's who I am."

REFLECTION QUESTIONS

How well do you participate in the celebration of the Eucharist? What would help you participate more consciously and actively?

How do you carry and share the presence of Christ you have received with those you spend time with on a daily basis? Would the people who see you daily be able to share many stories of ways in which you have been a light—of hope, forgiveness, understanding, care, service—for them?

Who are the disenfranchised, outcasts and forgotten in your circle of friends, family, work environment? Who are the disenfranchised, outcasts and forgotten in society today? How do you strive to be the presence of Christ for them?

ten

THÉRÈSE OF LISIEUX
mastering the art of true love

*But love your enemies, do good, and lend, expecting nothing in
return.*

—Luke 6:35a

When Thérèse of Lisieux died at the age of twenty-four, she was an
unknown nun from a Carmelite monastery in France. In the eyes of
most she had led a quiet and unremarkable life: a loving home, early
loss, early entry to religious life and an early death to tuberculosis. But
the autobiography that was published soon after her death revealed a
spiritual maturity beyond her years and a path to sanctity the world was
ready to embrace. Thérèse's was a path of love, a self-emptying love following in the footsteps of Jesus, a path built on the daily sacrifices of
choosing to generously and consciously express this love in the smallest
of actions.

early childhood loss
Thérèse was born in Alençon, France, on January 2, 1873, to Louis and
Zélie Martin, the youngest of five girls. Zélie was already sick with

terminal breast cancer and would pass away when Thérèse was four. After her death the sisters made the decision that from that day forward Thérèse would turn to Pauline (who was sixteen at the time) as her adoptive mother and Céline would turn to Marie (who was seventeen at the time).

The family moved to Lisieux where Zélie's brother Isidore and his wife could help Louis with the five girls. As much as Thérèse loved the time spent with her father walking around the town, and as much as she loved all her sisters, it was Pauline she grew closest to. When she was sick or afraid, it was Pauline to whom Thérèse turned; when she wanted permission to go places and do things, it was Pauline she asked; it was Pauline who began her educational instruction at home, who listened to Thérèse's worries and confidences, and, most importantly, who talked to Thérèse about a loving and merciful God.

When she was eight and a half, Thérèse began attending school at the Benedictine Abbey of Notre-Dame-du-Pre. Although a bright child, Thérèse was shy and socially unskilled at making friends and managing herself in this new social environment. Her classmates picked on her and she spent breaks alone. School was an entirely miserable experience and her home, her family—especially Pauline—became her refuge. She began to nurture a secret hope: to live a life apart with Pauline, in the desert. Pauline told Thérèse this was her dream too and

Pauline was very creative in her instruction says Thérèse: "One time I was expressing surprise that God should not give equal glory in heaven to all His elect, and I was afraid that everyone would not be happy. Then Pauline told me to go get Papa's big glass and to put it next to my little dice cup, and to fill them with water. Then she asked me which one was the most full. I told her that one was as full as the other and that it was impossible to put in more water than they could hold. Then my dear mother helped me understand that in Heaven, God would give to His elect as much glory as they could hold, and so the last would have nothing to envy about the first."[29]

that she was only waiting for Thérèse to be old enough, a response that heartened Thérèse.

But soon Thérèse learned that Pauline's dream was not quite what she had in mind. When Thérèse was nine, Pauline entered the Carmelite monastery in Lisieux, news that stunned Thérèse, who felt she was losing her mother all over again. As a result of this new loss, Thérèse came to the realization that life is "only suffering and continual separation,"[30] a harsh view for a child but one in keeping with her experiences. Seeing Pauline in Carmel also led Thérèse to reshape her dream by identifying the Carmelite monastery with her desert.

Thérèse's time with Pauline was now reduced to weekly half-hour visits, which she shared with the rest of the family. During these short visits Thérèse usually had very little one-on-one time with Pauline. The combination of this new separation, the visits to Carmel and school and her the loss of her mother, were too much for Thérèse and her health began to deteriorate. It began with headaches and chills; soon seizures, frightening hallucinations and even paralysis followed. The doctor was perplexed and could only diagnose hysteria. There was nothing that could be done and Louis feared his daughter was going crazy.

Weeks passed with few signs of improvement. Finally, one time when Marie heard Thérèse moaning in her room, she checked in on her and found her in such a state that she feared for her life. Desperate, Marie knelt before the statue of the Blessed Virgin Mary that was in the room and prayed for help. Her prayer was miraculously answered. Thérèse's gaze focused on the statue and she saw Mary smile at her; her symptoms disappeared, and Thérèse was at peace.

first steps on the spiritual journey

A year later, her health restored, Thérèse prepared for the next step in her spiritual journey: receiving her First Communion. While the nuns and priests taught her the catechism, Marie, and especially Pauline, who had prepared her for her first reconciliation, taught her the meaning of the sacrament and the path of holiness. Pauline wrote to her weekly and gave her a small book in which to inscribe the sacrifices—good deeds and acts of love she referred to as "flowers"—Thérèse did in preparation for the gift of the Eucharist. When the day of Thérèse's First Communion arrived, the experience surpassed all of her expectations. She described Communion as "a fusion" with Christ in which she felt herself to be freely and completely loved. Thérèse's joy was compounded by her experience of union not only with Christ, but through Christ, union with her mother and with her beloved Pauline.

Uneventful months passed by until approximately a year later when Thérèse went on a retreat at the Abbey. This retreat set her on a path of anxious self-recrimination and remorseful guilt. The retreat director terrified Thérèse with his excessive emphasis on sin and the importance of scrupulous confession of sins. Unable to let go of the priest's words, Thérèse began to see sin in every thought and deed, and felt compelled to confess every minor perceived infraction to Marie, who had taken charge of her upbringing. Given that Thérèse was experiencing the normal changes and emotional early-teen outbursts, there were many instances of "impure" thoughts and unkind words and actions. But Marie had a sensible head on her shoulders and persistently showed Thérèse these were normal thoughts and actions that she was distorting into sins through her own fears and tricks of the mind.

Soon Marie announced she too would enter the Carmelite monastery. The news cast a gloomy shadow over Thérèse as she entered the Christmas season, but the season of light would bring about a radical change in her. When the family returned from Christmas Eve Mass, Louis saw the shoes Thérèse had left out for him to fill with goodies.

Years later Céline also entered Carmel, bringing with her a camera. The pictures she took of the nuns in their daily activities provide a wonderful portrait of their days. Upon Thérèse's death, Céline used one of her pictures to make a portrait of Thérèse, and eventually added the details through which she became known as the "Little Flower."

Not realizing she could hear him, he expressed his relief that it was the last year. Hurt by these words, Thérèse rushed to her room. Normally she would have cried and agonized over the unintended injury for the rest of the evening, but that Christmas, that moment, Thérèse experienced a transformation. She realized she was not a child anymore and found the strength to do what she had never done before: put aside her hurt feelings in order to make someone else happy—in this case her father. Thérèse swallowed her tears, smiled,

In her autobiographical *Story of A Soul,* Thérèse expresses her ardent struggle to grasp her vocation. She describes a desire to be everything—a priest, an apostle, a martyr—before recognizing that "*Love* contains all the Vocations.... I cried out; 'Oh, Jesus, my Love...I have finally found my vocation: My vocation is Love!"[31] Her vocation found, Thérèse made it her purpose to show her love through actions, however small, confident that God would enable her to fulfill this lofty desire.

went downstairs as if nothing had happened and opened her gifts, joyfully making her father laugh as she did. This small moment was a life-changing one for Thérèse, one that ended the second phase of her life and opened the door to the third phase, in which her understanding of the meaning of love deepened and matured.

the road to carmel

Through prayer, reflection, spiritual reading and reading on other subjects, Thérèse's interior life slowly began to blossom. As her thoughts turned to the question of her vocation, she became convinced she had a call to the religious life, a call she felt so intensely that she wanted to be in the Carmelite convent by Christmas, the anniversary of her conversion. Utterly confident this was God's will for her, she began the uphill struggle to fulfill this vocation. She first told Marie, who thought she was too young, and then Pauline, who was receptive to the news and believed Thérèse truly did have a vocation. The next step was telling Louis. Louis had suffered a mild stroke only four weeks prior, and his daughters were understandably concerned about how the news would impact him. It was a Sunday afternoon and Louis was in the garden. Thérèse cried as she told him she wanted to enter Carmel by Christmas. Louis also shed some tears, but then gave Thérèse his blessing and became her greatest supporter.

Of their conversation in the garden, Thérèse recalls the following exchange with her father: "he showed me some *little white flowers*...and taking one of those flowers, he gave it to me, explaining to me with what care God had caused it to grow and had preserved it until that day.... [A]nd I saw that by trying to pick it Papa had pulled up all its *roots* without breaking them. It seemed destined to live on in another piece of ground, more fertile than the tender moss in which its first mornings had been spent."[32]

This difficult moment past her, Thérèse believed all that remained was to gain her uncle's support and the road to Carmel would be clear. But after Pauline gained his approval on her sister's behalf, they discovered one final impediment: According to the order's constitutions, a candidate had to be at least sixteen to enter the cloister. Only the ecclesiastical superior could approve an exception, and the superior was not inclined to do so.

Anxious to have the matter resolved quickly, Louis and Thérèse presented her case to the bishop, hoping to convince him to grant the permission the superior had denied. But the bishop wasn't prepared to make a hasty decision, and they had to head out on their scheduled pilgrimage to Rome without a clear answer.

During the trip, the future was never far from Thérèse's mind. Having so far been unsuccessful at obtaining a dispensation to enter Carmel, Thérèse was determined to make her case to the pope himself. The moment of truth arrived when it was Thérèse's turn to greet him and receive his blessing. Thérèse grabbed his knees and uttered the words she had practiced in anticipation of this moment: "Most Holy Father, I have a great grace to ask of you!... Most Holy Father...in honor of your jubilee, allow me to enter Carmel at the age of fifteen!..." Pope Leo XIII was old and almost completely deaf and had to turn to someone to ask what Thérèse had said. Briefed on her situation, the pope said to Thérèse, "Well, my child...do what the superiors tell you." Thérèse pressed, "Oh! Most Holy Father, if you were to say yes, everyone would be willing!..." Then the pope said, "All right.... All right.... *You will enter if it is God's will.*"[33] Thérèse remained frozen in place until finally carried away sobbing without the definitive answer she had hoped for.

Back home again Thérèse wrote one last letter to the bishop, knowing his vicar general had promised his help and support. When the bishop's reply finally arrived, it was to grant Thérèse's request. But before she could enter Carmel, one final and unexpected hurdle emerged. Pauline, concerned that Thérèse would be unable to keep the lenten observance, withdrew her support and requested she not enter until after Easter. Louis was furious; Thérèse was disappointed, but prepared to wait.

She did not waste the time she had to wait but pursued the lenten observances in her own way. Traditionally, the lenten observances were understood as self-imposed suffering, offered up for the good of others. Thérèse reinterpreted this practice to suit what she

During their tour of Rome, Thérèse discovered there were many places where women were forbidden entrance, a new experience for her: "I still can't understand why women are so easily excommunicated in Italy. At every moment we were told, 'Don't come in here....' 'Don't go in there, you would be excommunicated!...' Oh! Poor women, how they are disparaged!... In heaven He'll know how to show that His thoughts are not man's thoughts (Isa. 55:8-9), because then the *last* will be the *first* (Mt. 20:16).... More than once during the trip, I didn't have the patience to wait for heaven in order to be the first."[34]

Louis suffered a stroke in October 1888. Later, he seemed to also be experiencing hallucinations. Concerned he might become a danger to himself and others, Isidore institutionalized him in a mental hospital. It was heartbreaking for his daughters to know that their kindly and gentle father was deteriorating in such a place, especially because they did not believe he belonged there. He returned to Lisieux in May 1892 when death was near, an end that came two years later.

perceived as her particular challenge: "My mortifications consisted in breaking my will, which was always so ready to impose itself; in holding my tongue instead of answering back; in doing little things for others without hoping to get anything in return; in not slumping back when I was sitting down; etc., etc...."[35] In the years to come Thérèse would continue to deepen and develop her understanding of this path and in time began calling it "the little way."

Thérèse finally entered Carmel on March 9, 1888, at the age of fifteen. She took the habit in January of the following year and made her final vows that September. When she did, she took the opportunity to add the "and of the Holy Face" to her religious name "Thérèse of the Child Jesus." Now a full member of the community, despite the harshness of monastic life, Thérèse was happy.

the "little way" of love

In Carmel Thérèse seized every opportunity that presented itself to continue the path of self-emptying she had begun the Lent before entering the monastery. She regarded this path of self-sacrifice as a way to follow Jesus' command to love others as he has loved us. And contrary to what many may think, the monastery presented many opportunities for her to make these sacrificial acts of love. Her greatest challenge was one of the sisters who grated on her and on many of the other nuns. Rather than avoiding her, Thérèse made it a point to spend time with her and be kind to her, biting back the remarks she sometimes was tempted to say. Her purpose was always to let go of her need to impose her will upon others and act instead out love for Christ and a sincere desire to grow

After one occasion in Carmel when the sisters had been reminiscing about their childhood, Pauline asked Thérèse to write these stories down since she had such a good memory. Her work became the first part of her autobiography, *Story of a Soul*. Originally published with the announcement of Thérèse's death, interest in the book grew quickly and the Lisieux community could barely keep up with the requests for copies. Eight years after her death it had been translated into nine languages.

in this love, regardless of what others thought of her or how they judged her and interpreted her actions.

Inspired by reading John of the Cross and the lives of the saints, Thérèse wanted to become a saint herself, not just a saint, but a great saint. But she doubted such a goal was feasible for someone like her, so weak, of such an ordinary life: She fell asleep during Mass, she could hardly finish her assigned chores, she experienced doubts about her faith, and she struggled not to explode with the nipping daily irritations from her fellow nuns. Even though everything suggested her dream might be out of her reach, Thérèse persevered as she always had. She remained focused on her hope and continued to pursue it by following the "little way" she had been developing, the path of doing all things and bearing all things with love, eventually expressing her commitment with a prayer she called an Act of Oblation to God's Merciful Love.

"(W)hen someone asks nicely, it doesn't cost me to give, but if unfortunately they don't use delicate enough words, instantly the soul revolts if it isn't set firmly on charity. It finds a thousand reasons to refuse what is asked of it, and it's only after having convinced the asker of her lack of refinement that it finally gives *by grace* what she's asking for, or that it give her a light service that would have required twenty times less time to fulfill than it took to lay claim to imaginary rights."[36]

Thérèse continued her seemingly uneventful life in this manner until she coughed up blood for the first time when she was twenty-three. Only the prioress and Thérèse's doctor knew about the ailment, and unfortunately, the doctor didn't diagnose Thérèse's tuberculosis accurately and she declined without proper care. In addition, life at Carmel was hard and always had been. She had never complained, but the hardship must have taken an additional toll on her health.

Upon seeing the evidence of what would surely be an early death, Thérèse initially reacted with joy, confident in her faith and looking forward to being in heaven. But her joy was soon replaced by an agonizing doubt that death would only bring nothingness, that her faith was in vain, and she wrestled with this doubt as death drew near.

As Thérèse's story became known, the overwhelming worldwide acclamation of her holiness prompted the church to initiate an investigation into her cause only five years after her death. Pope Pius XI celebrated her canonization on May 17, 1925. She is the patron saint of missions, florists, tuberculosis sufferers, France, South Africa and numerous dioceses.

By April of the following year, Thérèse's symptoms were becoming more serious and impeding her ability to keep the rule. By May she was relieved of all her duties. She rallied in July, but essentially, there was nothing anyone could do. Despite her own crises of faith as she approached her death, Thérèse managed to cheer the saddened faces of visitors, making them laugh as usual and writing beautiful prayers for those who asked for them. Thérèse's final weeks were agonizingly painful, enough to make her comment: "If I had not had any faith, I would have committed suicide without an instant's hesitation"[37] and to request that medication not be left within her reach lest she reach for it in a moment of weakness. She died with the nuns gathered around her on September 30, 1897, at the age of twenty-four, an unknown nun most thought had led a rather unremarkable life.

REFLECTION
love

When it comes to love, loving and being loved, most of us probably expect and demand some reciprocity. Most of us probably also expect that reciprocity to take a particular shape that fits our understanding of what love looks like, sounds like and feels like in action. When Thérèse reflected on the meaning of love, loving and being loved, she looked to our greatest example, the example of Jesus, who was willing to lay down his life for us. She recognized that we are not called simply to love others because they reciprocate our love as we expect and demand they do.

Rather, we are called to a sacrificial, abundant, no-strings-attached kind of love, to a godly love.

When reflecting on what this love should look like, Thérèse was very practical: Love is actions—without them, there is no love. And these actions do not have to be grand gestures, simply the small, ordinary actions of our daily lives—moving a chair for an elderly and hard-to-please nun, letting someone else get a treat in her place, biting her tongue. The important thing is that these actions be done out of true love. Being truly loving means doing all those thankless tasks we do for others without complaining about the fact that they are thankless. It is not that there is anything wrong with recognition and gratitude. The difference lies in our own attitude. When we seek recognition for our actions, our action is no longer purely about loving the other person, but about the other person knowing what we have done and maybe even about winning some "you owe me" points we can cash in later.

the challenges

For some of us the thought of such humble and generous love is a little frightening. We may fear that unless we draw attention to the things we do, they may go unnoticed, and if they go unnoticed *we* may go unnoticed. That may indeed happen. When Thérèse was dying, some of the sisters wondered what the prioress would say about her because there didn't seem to be much one could say about Thérèse, except that she was, well, Thérèse. In a culture that admires celebrities, who wants to risk blending into the background as Thérèse did? We want to stand out, be admired for what we do, especially by those we love, and to do so while we're alive to enjoy it. But seeking such recognition encourages us to be self-centered, to focus on our image and how we're perceived. And as we become our own focus, we lose our ability to see others and with it our capacity to truly love them.

We may also fear that practicing such a kind of love will turn us into a doormat, which we all know means poor self-esteem, lack of assertiveness, insecurity and so on. Being the one who always calls, always plans get-togethers or trips, always picks up the slack, is always willing to adjust or make changes to help someone out might make us look like a doormat to others. But when those actions are the fruit of our conscious choice to be loving rather than our inability to make or express any other choice, we are not doormats. On the contrary, we are strong enough to make a choice we know might be misinterpreted because despite what everyone else may think or say, we know this is the way to our best self, the self that is patterned after Christ.

loving the challenging

Finally, lest we be tempted to interpret such love as directed only toward those who care for us, Jesus specifically calls us to love those who persecute us, and Thérèse was well aware of this call and its challenge in her daily life. For her, this translated into spending time with and being particularly helpful to the sister in the community she least cared for, the one who grated on her the most, knowing that it was Jesus she was helping. We all have such a person in our lives—it may be a friend, a coworker, a client, a relative—the person whose calls we try to avoid because if we don't we'll get trapped into listening to her latest saga, or coerced into helping with her chores, or embroiled in her latest scheme. We never know why we put up with it, except that in a small corner of our minds we know that person needs us. We may get trapped occasionally, and that's alright, but we don't go out of our way to spend more time with this person. Imagine making it a point to actually go out of our way to check up on this person, offering our help rather than waiting for that dreaded moment when we grit our teeth and swallow the comment as they ask for our help. Such is the love Jesus challenges us to live.

If such people are challenging to love, the mean-spirited, self-centered, self-absorbed ones in whom it is truly difficult to see the good are even harder. Unfortunately, we all run in to someone like that at some point too: the one who spreads malicious rumors about us, who tries to undermine our authority, sabotage our work or our relationship, the one who treats us as if our sole purpose in life were to cater to his every demand and should we fail to accommodate him threaten to go over our head. How can we treat someone like this with love when we can feel the bile rising within us when we see them, and we just want to throttle them and give them a piece of our mind? There is no easy answer to this one either. They too are children of God whom we are called to love and be kind to. Challenging as this is, God calls us to try, to make an effort, to at least not be mean back, knowing as Thérèse did, that the sacrifices we make in this life will pale in comparison to the eternal reward Christ has won for us through his.

Real love, loving as Jesus loved, is not something that just happens to us. Loving is a conscious choice, an active discipline of letting go of our need to impose our will on others and becoming other-centered as Thérèse did. Thérèse devoted herself to becoming truly loving, making it her single purpose. If we employ a fraction of Thérèse's dedication, we will be well on our way as well.

REFLECTION QUESTIONS

What does love mean to you? What does it mean to be a loving person? Who are the people in your life who are good examples of what it means to be a loving person?

How are you a loving person? Do your actions and words express the kind of generous and selfless love Jesus exemplifies? What holds you back from being more loving?

What motivates your actions for others? The hope of recognition? The expectation the favor will be returned? Real love and care for them and their well-being?

How do you treat those you find irritating, selfish or mean-spirited? Do you make an effort to be kind?

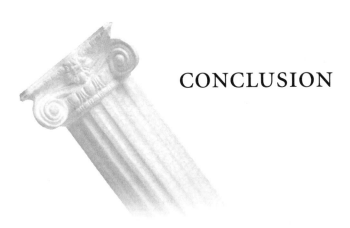

CONCLUSION

And so we come to the end of this brief glimpse into the lives of some of the great heroes of our faith. As I look back upon the lives of these saints, there are several themes I see that recur time and time again. Most important among them is the fact that they all wanted to be holy, they all worked hard and put effort into becoming men and women of integrity, into leading lives of purpose and meaning, reflecting in their actions and words the gospel message they had received. Holiness didn't just magically happen to them by some accident of fate; holiness was a goal they set for themselves, one they prayed and worked to reach.

The church tells us we are all called to holiness, to become saints, that we should all set this goal for ourselves. I wonder how many of us are bold enough to do so. To admit, even to ourselves, that our heart's desire is to become saints might seem a little—or very—arrogant. But none of these stories reveal arrogant people. On the contrary, holiness by definition demands humility born of the recognition that it is not we who make ourselves holy, but God who brings this work about in us, radiating God's very life through us. And if saints are who we are truly called to be, then how can it be arrogant to aspire to become who we are meant to be?

Perhaps rather than arrogant, aspiring to holiness today still appears to many as an enterprise reserved for the overly pious among us, not for ordinary, flawed people such as ourselves. When such thoughts dissuade us and tempt us to be content with a mediocre attempt at responding to God's love for us, we would do well to remember the stories of the saints. All of them could have chosen to be satisfied with being "good enough" at various points in their lives. If they had, their lives would indeed have been "good" as ours are. But they were not willing to respond half-heartedly to God's boundless love for us, and, despite the challenges and struggles, they continued to strive to be ever more Christ-like, to surrender more fully to God in service to the world. It is this determination to persevere that set them above others, and it is this determination we are called to embrace.

Holiness is for all of us. We may not all be capable of becoming great athletes, brilliant scientists, financial wizards or successful businesspeople. But we are all capable of responding to God's love for us by using the gifts we do have, in the context in which we find ourselves, with passion, devotion and purpose. The challenge for us is the same one faced by the saints: the challenge to make it a priority and devote time and effort to growing in holiness—today, tomorrow and each day. Yet we are blessed in that we do not start from scratch. Rather, we stand on the shoulders of these great saints who have gone before us, men and women to whom we can look for inspiration as we embark and persevere on this journey, as well as for a wealth of guidance as to spiritual practices that might help us on our way.

As we contemplate the path we are called to follow, I invite you to do so, carrying with you these words from the Letter to the Hebrews:

> Therefore, since we are surrounded by so great a cloud of witnesses, let us also lay aside every weight and the sin that clings so closely, and let us run with perseverance the race that is set

before us, looking to Jesus the pioneer and perfecter of our faith, who for the sake of the joy that was set before him endured the cross, disregarding its shame, and has taken his seat at the right hand of the throne of God. (12:1–2)

BIBLIOGRAPHY

PETER

Malina, Bruce J. *The New Testament World: Insights from Cultural Anthropology, revised edition.* Louisville, Ky.: Westminster/John Knox, 1993.

Perkins, Pheme. *Peter: Apostle for the Whole Church.* Minneapolis: Augsburg Fortress, 2000.

Reiser, William. *Talking About Jesus Today: An Introduction to the Story Behind Our Story.* New York: Paulist, 1993.

Willig, Jim and Tammy Bundy. *A Retreat with Peter: Growing from Sinner to Saint.* Cincinnati: St. Anthony Messenger, 2001.

AUGUSTINE OF HIPPO

Augustine. *Confessions: Books I-XIII*, F.J. Sheed, trans. Indianapolis: Hackett, 1993.

———. *Sermons to the People: Advent, Christmas, New Year's, Epiphany*, William Griffin, trans. and ed. New York: Image, 2002.

Brown, Peter. *Augustine of Hippo: A Biography, revised edition.* Berkeley, Calif.: University of California Press, 2000.

Lancel, Serge. *Saint Augustine*, Antonia Nevill, trans. London: SCM, 2002.

FRANCIS OF ASSISI

Cunningham, Lawrence S. *Francis of Assisi: Performing the Gospel Life.* Grand Rapids: Eerdmans, 2004.

Frugoni, Chiara. *Francis of Assisi: A Life*, John Bowden, trans. New York: Continuum, 1998.

House, Adrian. *Francis of Assisi: A Revolutionary Life.* New York: Paulist, 2003.

CATHERINE OF SIENA

Catherine of Siena. *Passion for the Truth, Compassion for Humanity: selected spiritual writings*, Mary O'Driscoll, O.P., ed. Hyde Park, N.Y.: New City, 1993.

———. *The Dialogue (Classics of Western Spirituality)*, Suzanne Noffke, O.P., trans. New York: Paulist, 1980.

Flinders, Carol Lee. *Enduring Grace: Living Portraits of Seven Women Mystics.* New York: HarperSanFrancisco, 1993.

Giordani, Igino. *Saint Catherine of Siena—Doctor of the Church*, Thomas J. Tobin, trans. Boston: Daughters of St. Paul, 1980.

Noffke, Suzanne. *Catherine of Siena: Vision through a Distant Eye.* Collegeville, Minn.: Liturgical, 1996.

Raymond of Capua. *The Life of Catherine of Siena*, Conleth Kearns, O.P., trans. Wilmington, Del.: Michael Glazier, 1980.

TERESA OF AVILA

Du Boulay, Shirley. *Teresa of Avila: An Extraordinary Life.* New York: BlueBridge, 1991.

Luti, J. Mary. *Teresa of Avila's Way.* Collegeville, Minn.: Liturgical, 1991.

Teresa of Avila. *The Interior Castle*, Mirabai Starr, trans. New York: Riverhead, 2003.

———. *The Life of Teresa of Jesus: The Autobiography of Teresa of Avila*, E. Allison Peers, trans. and ed. New York: Image, 1991.

———. *The Way of Perfection*, E. Allison Peers, trans. and ed. New York: Image, 1991.

ALOYSIUS GONZAGA

Cepari, Virgilio. *The Life of St. Aloysius Gonzaga, of the Company of Jesus*, Edward Healy Thompson, ed. Philadelphia: P.F. Cunningham, 1867.

Martindale, C.C., S.J. *The Vocation of Aloysius Gonzaga.* London: Sheed and Ward, 1929.

MARTIN DE PORRES

Cavallini, Giuliana. *St. Martin de Porres: Apostle of Charity*, Caroline Holland, trans. St. Louis: B. Herder, 1963.

Kearns, J.C., O.P. *The Life of Blessed Martin de Porres: Saintly American Negro and Patron of Social Justice.* New York: P.J. Kenedy and Sons, 1937.

ELIZABETH ANN SETON

Celeste, Marie, S.C. *Elizabeth Ann Seton: A Self-Portrait (1774-1821).* Libertyville, Ill.: Franciscan Marytown, 1986.

Dirvin, Joseph I., C.M. *Mrs. Seton: Foundress of the American Sisters of Charity.* New York: Farrar, Straus and Cudahy, 1962.

Seton, Robert, D.D., ed. *Memoir, Letters and Journal, of Elizabeth Seton, Convert to the Catholic Faith, and Sister of Charity.* 2 vols. New York: P. O'Shea, 1869.

White, Charles I. *Mother Seton: Mother of Many Daughters,* Sisters of Charity of Mount St. Vincent-on-Hudson, eds. Garden City, N.Y.: Doubleday, 1949.

KATHARINE DREXEL

Baldwin, Lou. *Saint Katharine Drexel: Apostle to the Oppressed.* Philadelphia: The Catholic Standard and Times, 2000.

O'Brien, Felicity. *Treasure in Heaven.* Middlegreen, United Kingdom: St. Paul, 1991.

Van Balen Holt, Mary. *Meet Katharine Drexel: Heiress and God's Servant of the Oppressed.* Ann Arbor, Mich.: Charis, 2002.

THÉRÈSE OF LISIEUX

Bro, Bernard. *Saint Thérèse of Lisieux: Her Family, Her God, Her Message,* Anne Englund Nash, trans. San Francisco: Ignatius, 1996.

Flinders, Carol Lee. *Enduring Grace: Living Portraits of Seven Women Mystics.* New York: HarperSanFrancisco, 1993.

Laforest, Ann, O.C.D. *Thérèse of Lisieux: the Way to Love.* Franklin, Wis.: Sheed and Ward, 2000.

O'Connor, Patricia. *Thérèse of Lisieux: A Biography.* Huntington, Ind.: Our Sunday Visitor, 1983.

Thérèse of Lisieux. *The Story of A Soul, A New Translation,* Robert J. Edmonson, C.J., trans. and ed. Brewster, Mass.: Paraclete, 2006.

———. *St. Thérèse of Lisieux, Her Last Conversations,* John Clarke, O.C.D., trans. Washington, D.C.: ICS, 1977.

NOTES

1. Augustine, *Confessions,* F.J. Sheed, trans. (Indianapolis: Hackett, 1993), p. 18.

2. Augustine, p. 26.

3. Augustine, p. 55.

4. Augustine, p. 139.

5. Augustine, p. 146.

6. Francis, of Assisi, *Testament,* quoted in Lawrence S. Cunningham, *Francis of Assisi: Performing the Gospel Life* (Grand Rapids: Eerdmans, 2004), p. 9.

7. E. Allison Peers, trans. and ed., *The Life of Teresa of Jesus: The Autobiography of Teresa of Avila* (New York: Image, 1991), p. 112.

8. Peers, pp. 219–220.

9. Peers, pp. 274–275.

10. Giuliana Cavallini, *St. Martin de Porres: Apostle of Charity,* Caroline Holland, trans. (St. Louis: B. Herder, 1963), p. 12.

11. Robert Seton, D.D., ed., *Memoir, Letters and Journal, of Elizabeth Seton, Convert to the Catholic Faith, and Sister of Charity,* vol. 2 (New York: P. O'Shea, 1869), p. 148.

12. Seton, vol. 2, p. 151.

13. Robert Seton, D.D., ed., *Memoir, Letters and Journal, of Elizabeth Seton, Convert to the Catholic Faith, and Sister of Charity,* vol. 1 (New York: P. O'Shea, 1869), p. 87.

14. Seton, vol. 1, pp. 88–89.

15. Seton, vol. 1, p. 126.

16. Seton, vol. 1, p. 134.

17. Seton, vol. 1, p. 145.

18. Seton, vol. 1, p. 211.

19. Charles I. White, *Mother Seton: Mother of Many Daughters,* Sisters of Charity of Mount St. Vincent-on-Hudson, New York, eds., (Garden City, N.Y.: Doubleday, 1949), p. 225.

20. White, p. 222.

21. Archives of the Daughters of Charity, Eastern Province, St. Joseph's Central House, Emmitsburg, Md., VI, 91, quoted in Joseph I. Dirvin, C.M., *Mrs. Seton: Foundress of the American Sisters of Charity* (New York: Farrar, Straus and Cudahy, 1962), p. 320.

22. Archives of the Daughters of Charity, Eastern Province, St. Joseph's Central House, Emmitsburg, Md., VII, 49, quoted in Dirvin, p. 321, quoting Luke 23:46.

23. Lou Baldwin, *Saint Katharine Drexel: Apostle to the Oppressed* (Philadelphia: The Catholic Standard and Times, 2000), p. 2.

24. Bishop O'Connor to Katharine Drexel, February 28, 1889, in *Archives, Sisters of the Blessed Sacrament,* as quoted in Baldwin, p. 71.

25. Annals, *Archives, Sisters of the Blessed Sacrament,* as quoted Baldwin, p. 89.

26. *Positio* relating to the cause of Katharine Drexel, 8, as quoted in Felicity O'Brien, *Treasure in Heaven* (Middlegreen, United Kingdom: St. Paul, 1991), p. 114.

27. *Positio,* vol. I, 517, as quoted in O'Brien, p. 81.

28. *Positio,* vol II, 118, as quoted in Baldwin, p. 155.

29. Thérèse of Lisieux, *The Story of A Soul: A New Translation,* Robert J. Edmonson, C.J., trans. (Brewster, Mass.: Paraclete, 2006), pp. 40–41.

30. Thérèse of Lisieux, p. 55.

31. Thérèse of Lisieux, p. 217.

32. Thérèse of Lisieux, p. 117.

33. Thérèse of Lisieux, pp. 151–152.

34. Thérèse of Lisieux, p. 159.

35. Thérèse of Lisieux, p. 164.

36. Thérèse of Lisieux, pp. 254–255.

37. Thérèse of Lisieux, *St. Thérèse of Lisieux, Her Last Conversations*, John Clarke, O.C.D, trans. (Washington, D.C.: ICS, 1977), p. 196.